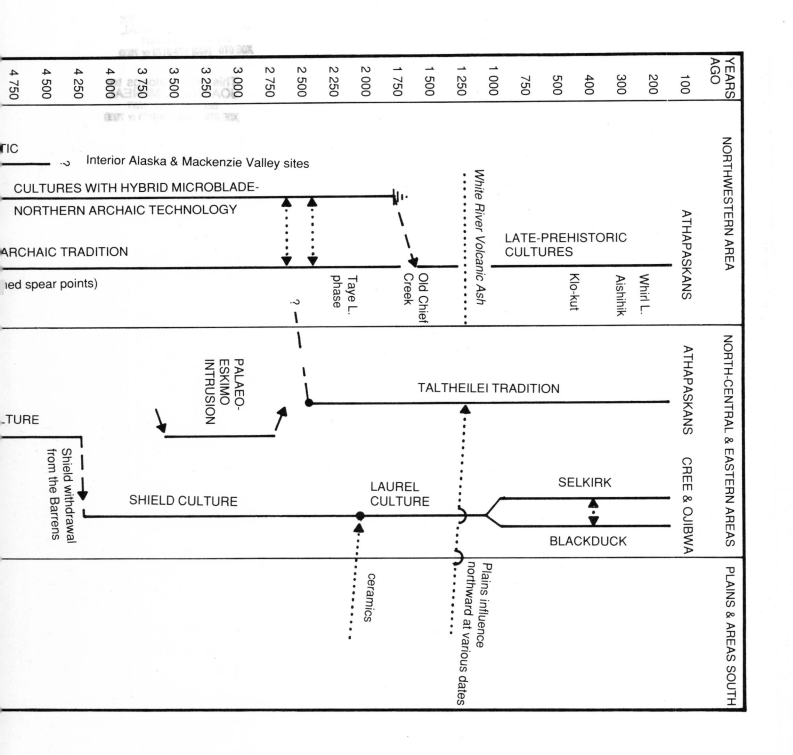

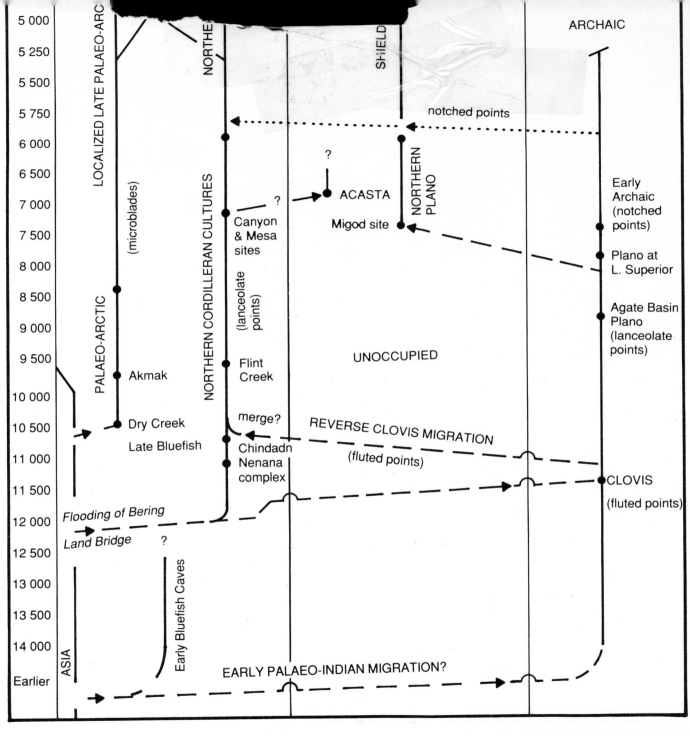

Cultural Chronology of Subarctic Prehistory

Continuity through time	——————
Migration	– – – – –
Diffusion or Influence	··············

Western Subarctic Prehistory

Canadian Prehistory Series

A growing interest in Canadian prehistory and the introduction of new archaeological techniques have resulted in significant discoveries across Canada. This series enables the general reader to enjoy for the first time a popular account of these exciting new findings in Canadian prehistory. Each book explores the prehistory of a particular geographical or cultural area, and the authors, who are leading scholars in their field, describe many fascinating aspects of archaeological research. Time charts, graphs, maps and numerous photographs and drawings recreate a vivid picture of the life of the native peoples in Canada before Jacques Cartier.

Western Subarctic Prehistory

Donald W. Clark

Archaeological Survey of Canada
Canadian Museum of Civilization
Hull, Quebec

CANADIAN CATALOGUING IN PUBLICATION DATA

Clark, Donald W.
    Western subarctic prehistory

(Canadian prehistory series)
Includes bibliographical references.
ISBN 0-660-12920-5

1. Northwest, Canadian — Antiquities. 2. Arctic regions — Antiquities. 3. Indians of North America — Antiquities. I. Archaeological Survey of Canada. II. Canadian Museum of Civilization. III. Title. IV. Series.

E78.C2C52   1991   971.9'01   C91-098672-X

Printed and bound in Canada

Published by the
Canadian Museum of Civilization
Hull, Quebec
J8X 4H2

Photographs of Artifacts: Richard Garner
Project Manager: Catherine Cunningham-Huston
Maps and Drawings: David Laverie
Layout: Francine Boucher
Printing Coordinator: Deborah Brownrigg
Cover Design: Purich Design Studio

Cover: Great Bear Lake, NWT
Inset: This fine example of a lance blade was found in 1882 at Fond-du-Lac, Lake Athabasca, in what is now northern Saskatchewan.

Contents

List of Illustrations

Maps

Preface

The Western Subarctic undoubtedly contains the oldest record of human occupation of the Americas. To find that record and identify that moment in New World prehistory must be the ambition of every North American archaeologist, particularly those of us whose specialty is the Subarctic. The traces of these first settlers have been largely erased by time and Ice Age glaciers, but we know that some of the newcomers stayed in the North, while others continued to move southwards. The latter developed lifeways wholly unlike those of the Subarctic, but all were once apprentices to the North.

This eighth volume in the Canadian Prehistory Series tells the story of those who stayed on, who endured the harshness and knew the beauty of the Subarctic. Parts of the Canadian Subarctic were covered in earlier volumes of the series, particularly those on Ontario, Quebec, and Newfoundland/Labrador. To avoid duplication and to make a very complex subject more intelligible, the coverage of the present volume excludes most of the Eastern Subarctic.

Treatment of the topic is primarily regional, though there are also chapters on research methods and prehistoric trade. For the purposes of this study, Canada's Western Subarctic is divided into three regions, whose prehistories usually differ, though at times cultures spanned more than one region. Within each region, we will begin with the most ancient cultures and move forward in time.

As recently as twenty years ago, many parts of the Subarctic had received scant attention from archaeologists, and the prehistory of some areas remains barely known today. In attempting to arrive at a "big picture," it has been necessary to gloss over inadequacies, choose among conflicting interpretations, and cut detailed explanations short: Fortunately, I have been able to draw upon the ideas, hypotheses, interpretations and compilations of dozens of my colleagues and predecessors.

Preparation of this volume as well my fieldwork in the North have been wholly supported by the Canadian Museum of Civilization.

Introduction

The Area

This book is a prehistory of the Middle North, the region between the arctic and temperate zones of North America. While the Subarctic can be defined geographically, we will follow an ethnographic, or culture-area, approach but will restrict the actual area covered to give the book a primarily Canadian focus. There is a correlation between the environment of a region and the subsistence lifeways, clothing, types of housing, and modes of transportation of its inhabitants. On that basis, the map of tribal distribution for the Americas groups the numerous Native tribes into a small number of culture areas. The Subarctic is one of these areas.

Certain conventions enter into the definition of culture areas. For example, all Eskimos and Aleuts are assumed to inhabit the Arctic, though some of them occupy boreal-forest lands and others live along the temperate North Pacific coast. Conversely, a part of the Barren Grounds—generally considered an arctic environment—has been assigned to the Subarctic because the inhabitants at the time of historical contact were Indians. The people of a culture area are not always limited to a single linguistic family. The Subarctic is shared mainly by speakers of Athapaskan and Algonquian languages, whose homelands are in the Western and Eastern Subarctic respectively. Moreover, tribes of a single linguistic family have often diverged and adapted to different areas; for example, people of Athapaskan origin inhabit not only subarctic forests, but also the near-desert country of northern Mexico. Simply stated, our ethnographically based definition of the Subarctic refers primarily to the land of the boreal forest. Map 1 will be our final guide. We will hold to the same boundaries through time, despite the shifts that have occurred during the millennia in environment or vegetation and in tribal or linguistic populations. Chaos would result if we were to make the passage of time a factor in our definition of the Subarctic.

This book is not directly concerned with events that took place in the Alaskan subarctic, but as there were no national borders to separate native populations, Canadian prehistory cannot be studied without reference to Alaskan prehistory. Moreover, Alaskan data can be used to augment the archaeological evidence in Canada.

A deliberate geographical limitation was set on this work, confining it to the subarctic area west of Lake Superior and Hudson Bay

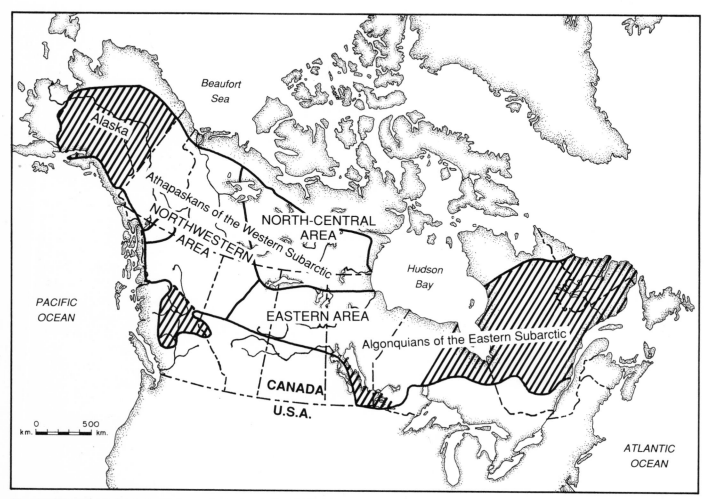

Map 1. The Western Subarctic as Defined in This Book The three areas—Northwestern, North-Central, and Eastern—described in the text are superimposed on the ethnographically based delineation of the Canadian Subarctic, which is divided into two major regions (termed the Eastern and Western Subarctic) on the basis of the distribution of the two main ethnic groups, the Athapaskans and Algonquians. The cross-hatched areas are those parts of the ethnographer's Subarctic that are not covered by this volume for reasons that are explained in the Introduction.

and phasing out gradually in Northern Ontario (Map 1). The rest of the Eastern Subarctic has been excluded because it was previously described in the Canadian Prehistory Series in the volumes on Quebec, Ontario, and Newfoundland/Labrador. Also excluded here is central-interior British Columbia, an environmentally complex region with an equally complex prehistory and populated by an array of Indian tribes; it was covered by this series in the volume on British Columbia. Thus, the approach followed here differs from that in some of the other volumes, which were defined by provincial boundaries.

In this volume, we follow prehistory onto the Barren Grounds and into the western mountains, but most of our time will be spent in the boreal forest. The landscape of the Subarctic is a complex of mountains, narrow valleys and uplands in the west, broad rivers and densely forested plains in the middle, and, in the east, the irregular rocky outcrops of the Canadian Shield, dotted with countless lakes and rushing rivers. Botanically, the south-to-north transition is from mixed-wood parkland to coniferous forests, or taiga, in the centre to the forest/tundra beyond, where trees struggle to exist in the approaches to the Barrens of the Far North (Map 2). Partway through this forest expanse, pine and certain shrubs abandon their attempt to vegetate the North. The Subarctic forest, where most of the archaeological finds occur, is a mosaic of small communities of different trees and small plants, and of shrub plains and extensive zones of muskeg. Muskeg reluctantly shares the lowlands with stunted black spruce and even invades higher slopes. Ribbons of poplars mark the courses of streams and rivers. Elsewhere, according to the dictates of plant succession, frequent forest fires and local growing conditions, mixed forests (poplar, birch and white spruce) or shrubbed plains predominate.

Canada's Western Subarctic contained not only diverse natural zones in the past, but there were major regional differences in prehistoric cultures and more than one linguistic group in the area. To organize this work in a manner that recognizes these differences without unduly complicating the story, I have divided our area of study into three regions, as shown on Map 1. The Northwestern Area is the largest, encompassing interior Alaska, both Territories east to Great Slave Lake, and northern British Columbia and Alberta. A second, which includes the southern Barren Grounds and the

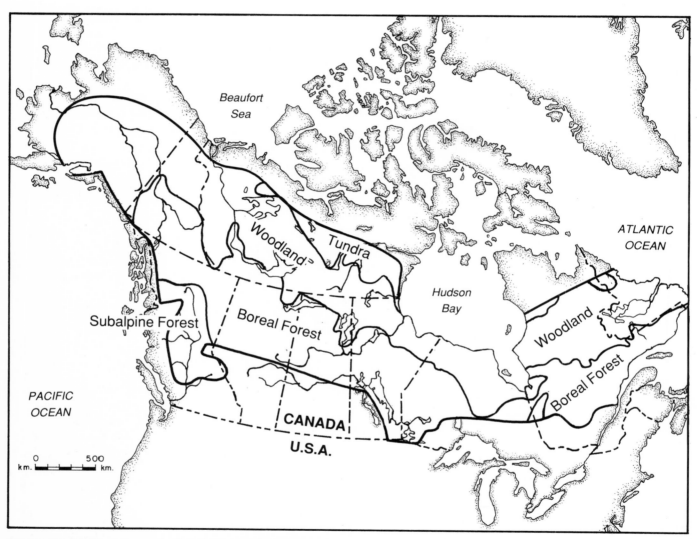

Beaufort
Sea

ATLANTIC
OCEAN

Woodland

Tundra

Hudson
Bay

Subalpine Forest

Boreal Forest

Woodland

PACIFIC
OCEAN

Boreal Forest

CANADA

U.S.A.

0   500
km.   km.

Map 2. Vegetation Zones in the Canadian Subarctic The line circumscribing the vegetation zones accords with the ethnographer's delineation of the Subarctic.

forest/tundra zone and lies close to the geographical centre of Canada, will be referred to here as the North-Central Area. In the third region, which I call the Eastern Area, the forest dwellers have been primarily Crees in historical times, but there were intermittent Athapaskan occupations at the northern edge during late prehistory. Our Eastern Area, extending out of the eastern subarctic of Ontario, across Manitoba and Saskatchewan and into central Alberta, is part of the larger region defined by ethnologists as the Eastern Subarctic.

History of Subarctic Archaeology

Today the Bering Strait separates North America from Asia. But when the glaciers covered much of North America, a broad ice-free plain connected Siberia to Alaska. From Asia came men and women into a new world. They moved eastwards into a grassy tundra region of interior Alaska–Yukon, called Beringia, alive with animals but blocked at times to the east and south by ice. They hunted with stone-tipped spears, skinned their prey with large bone flakes, and butchered with stone knives.

As the Ice Age ended, the glaciers melted, flooding the land-bridge, but new lands opened to the south. Some of the people moved on.
(*Voice text of a former exhibit of the Canadian Museum of Civilization*)

Initially, archaeological research in the Subarctic focused on the quest for evidence of early human migrations—the event described in the quotation above. At the end of the 1920s, the physical anthropologist Aleš Hrdlička was searching the banks of the Yukon River in Alaska. In the late 1930s, Froelich Rainey was surveying and excavating in central and eastern Alaska, recording whatever he found but intent on discovering evidence of early migration from Asia to North America. During this period there were other surveys with similar objectives, including one down the Mackenzie River valley to the Arctic Ocean that produced almost no results. By the beginning of the 1940s, the study of Subarctic prehistory was limited principally to the Campus site in Alaska and to several lesser finds that were difficult to interpret because they could not be related to prehistoric cultures elsewhere. The Campus site did provide evidence of early contact with Asia, but it involves a toolmaking technique now known to have lasted for several thousand years; the site is now thought to be only about 3 500 years old.

In 1944, archaeological field parties started to make frequent treks to the southern Yukon Territory, in 1949 to the Mackenzie Basin of the Northwest Territories, in 1955 to the northern Yukon, and finally, in 1958, to the southern Barrens of the Keewatin District. Interior Alaska received only sporadic attention until the 1960s, when the pace of fieldwork there quickened. The most persistent investigator was Richard S. MacNeish, who, on the basis of his hard-won findings, wrote highly speculative interpretations of Subarctic prehistory. The objective during this period continued to be to shed light on the peopling of the New World, although scientists observed and studied whatever they could find. Indeed, few of their findings had any bearing on the first settlers of the Americas.

Recovery of small and undated collections from sites spread over more than a million square kilometres, and partitioned among innumerable occupations from as far back as 12 000 years ago, left many questions of Subarctic prehistory unanswered, some areas unknown, and conclusions disputed. Many archaeologists have studied these problems, but with limited success as yet. Promising sites of known antiquity are so rare that few Subarctic archaeologists can devote their attention to a single period. It is far more common to focus on a relatively unknown area and direct attention to whatever finds are made. In recent decades, however, in the hope of using the knowns of history to apprehend prehistory, some researchers have focused on historical camps and villages that can be identified with specific Native peoples.

The Allure of Subarctic Prehistory

Given all the problems, why study Subarctic prehistory? To the intellectually adventurous, that question is akin to asking mountaineers why they climb mountains. Across its immensity the Subarctic offers the prospect of being tormented by insects, attacked by bears, rained on, and denied all the comforts of civilization. As a bonus, there is the very real joy to be found in the hunt for knowledge, in finding key evidence, and in interpreting the clues to events in the lives of ancient peoples.

The prehistory of the Subarctic is of particular interest to those who reflect on the state of humankind before urbanization and industrialization, and on how Native North Americans subsisted before the development of agricultural communities. All Native peoples of the Americas were once apprentices to the North. Those whose descendants were to build the cities and temples of Meso-America and Peru, discover metallurgy, and develop the cultivation of potatoes, tomatoes, maize and many other food staples were hunters and gatherers in the Subarctic when the New World was first being settled. Though many of the people moved on to southern lands, others stayed behind, and their tools lie awaiting discovery on frozen, wind-swept ridges. Perhaps they preferred to cope with a familiar, if exacting, environment than to venture into the unknown. Certainly, the skills to survive in the North had developed before the end of the Ice Age 10 000 years ago. Snow and frost were not enemies, but made it possible to traverse land, bogs and rivers with ease, to preserve game and fish against spoilage, and to track the animals that provided food and the materials for clothing and shelter.

But the animals were not always there. Seasonally, and sometimes unpredictably as well, vast reaches of the Subarctic were almost devoid of game. Even the fish moved to deeper waters to overwinter or were inaccessible under thick ice. A poor season or a wrong decision could result in disaster. In the Subarctic, the resources upon which hunter-fisher-gatherers depended could support only a sparse, mobile population. Agriculture or horticulture were impractical, though animal husbandry as practised in Siberia was theoretically possible. Technology was adapted to the need for mobility, and social organization to the sparseness of the population. Equipment and paraphernalia had to be light and portable, and housing temporary. Under these conditions, it was unlikely that people would form large, permanent settlements or strong political systems.

One might ask, then, if prehistoric cultures continued to develop much beyond the stage reached at the end of the Ice Age. Do the late-prehistoric cultures of the North and the inhabitants at the time of European contact manifest frozen development of an ancient lifeway that has been superseded in temperate zones? Which of their achievements are their own, and which are to be credited to outside sources? These questions cannot be answered conclusively, but we shall be able to demonstrate a long, complex and varied regional prehistory. Sometimes the people developed independently, and sometimes they depended on innovations made elsewhere. The future may even show that some elements of Native technology had a Subarctic genesis.

Discovering Subarctic Prehistory

In the chapters that follow we will see several thousand years of prehistory gradually unfold in the Subarctic. Historical accounts began with the arrival of Europeans, who explored the Subarctic and opened up the fur trade. Native contacts with Europeans increased by stages. Initially, only certain groups had access to the traders, and these Natives in turn became middlemen who bartered with tribes farther inland. Eventually, however, European trading posts were established in nearly every region. The twentieth century brought a much greater influx of non-Native residents, who have introduced a whole new range of activities, institutions and attitudes, and in the process weakened the remaining links with the past. The last few threads connecting today's northern hamlets with the camp-sites of prehistory have almost all been severed. To reconstruct these links requires the study of not only prehistory, but also the early years of the historical period.

In the Western Subarctic a faint voice still does rise almost directly from prehistory. There, until recently, the people lived close to the land, as their ancestors had. Their activities thus provide us with keys for interpreting, cautiously, the lives of their antecedents, whose tools and other remains we dig up and carefully preserve for study. Archaeology has thus become more a study of people than a fixation on objects from the past.

It is necessary to understand how material remains came to be discarded and to survive in the ground to form the archaeological record. In studying this record, archaeologists use an array of operational, intellectual and analytical tools for recovering, studying and interpreting prehistoric remains. With only fragmented, scattered data, they try to reconstruct the past and build a coherent picture of what went on in prehistory. Not until they have completed their tasks as technician, recorder and interpreter are archaeologists ready to tell the story their studies have revealed.

A Record Written on the Land

The resources on which life once depended in the Subarctic are subject to long periods of scarcity and abundance, further complicated by the effects of seasonal cycles. An example of the latter is the annual migration and dispersal of caribou, a cycle that occurs among many species. During times of scarcity, people either survived through a combination of skill and chance, or they starved. Often they starved, leaving vast regions virtually uninhabited. Survival required a seasonal round of travel and subsistence activities; even so, alternatives often had to be sought when preferred resources failed. When the people were not gathered for a communal hunt, for fishing or for ceremonial occasions, they had to scatter in families or small groups over the land. In the 1930s, one Athapaskan man described the round of activities as follows:

> In the old days … always they were on the trail, hunting and camping. In July whitefish were dried and cached at the Fish Camp. Then the people went moose hunting, caching the meat. In the winter they visited the caches and then when the caribou came they killed caribou. After the moose season the people went up to the head [of the river into the hills] to secure sheepskins for winter. Then they would return to the village; make their clothes; and then take the winter hunting trails…. In the spring when the leaves were coming out they returned to the village. They would take birch bark and sew it together to make new tents [rectangular summer houses] and then wait for the caribou to come back again. (Reported in Robert A. McKennan, *The Upper Tanana Indians*, Yale University Publications in Anthropology, No. 55 [1959]: 46.)

In the course of their activities, northern Natives have inadvertently left many cryptic clues to their lives on the land. At each camp a few traces of the band's presence remained after the people moved on. Patches of ash and charcoal mark the position of fires. Sometimes a hearth is surrounded by cobbles or stone slabs. At one camp a ring of stone tent-weights outlines the location of a temporary shelter. Flakes from the sharpening of a stone knife point to a work area at another, and some sites contain broken spear tips. Here and

Plate 1. Endscrapers These bits from a very common prehistoric tool—the stone endscraper—represent many periods and cultures. Flaked to a steep, blunt working edge at the rounded end and hafted in a short handle, endscrapers must have been employed for a variety of tasks, judging from their great size range. But the majority were probably used to scrape traces of flesh and fat off the underside of hides to be made into tents, clothing, bags, blankets and thongs. Some prehistoric cultures had very distinctive styles of endscrapers, but most were simple, generalized tools. The scraper at bottom left is 11.7 cm long.

there are bones discarded from dinners past, but after a century has elapsed, few traces remain of the occupants' brush shelters. Constantly on the move, people returned seasonally, time and again, to places where life had been successful. They disturbed the old traces and left new ones. Children made playhouses and, one can surmise, lost a stone scraper while surreptitiously using mother's implements. Adolescents learning to make tools left behind the products of their botched attempts. Sometimes, a pit was dug into the ground to provide cold storage for berries or fish. Gradually, with recurrent use, the most-frequented sites grew rich in discards scattered over a wide area. As if the message of the site, rewritten many times over before the camp fell into disuse, were not confusing enough, nature too has taken a hand in destroying the record.

Decay destroys wooden materials, bark baskets, shelters, skins, and other organic remains, while acid soils, the roots of growing plants, and calcium-craving rodents and porcupines soon begin to eradicate bone and antler tools and refuse. Forest fires may consume what these natural forces do not. Bears searching for grubs roll the tent weights about. Ground squirrels building their burrows below the surface and brown bears digging for the squirrels from above churn the soil as efficiently as a blender beats eggs. Frost action, soil creep and slope wash slowly disarrange the surviving stone tools, flaking debris, and hearths. Thus, even favoured locations where people must have camped and worked hundreds of times often yield only sparse traces. Most wraithlike of all are the camps that were built on frozen bogs, lakes and rivers; they usually sank without a trace every year at spring breakup.

Fortunately for archaeologists, floodwaters sometimes quickly sealed riverbank camps under layers of preserving silt. At others, the wind blew sand in from adjacent beaches and barren ridges, burying camp floors intact. Items in old caches and housepits were sometimes preserved as the pits filled in. These buried sites and the disturbed surface remains are what the archaeologist seeks out, "reads," and writes up as prehistory.

Exploring the Land

Ancient campsites and artifacts come to the attention of archaeologists in many ways. Sometimes the public discovers them by accident and reports them to museums, universities or government agencies. Archaeologists sometimes locate them by questioning local residents, collectors and lodge operators, as well as farmers in favoured parts of the Subarctic. However, by far the greatest number of sites are found by a direct search, called an *archaeological survey*. Surveying entails a lot of reconnaissance on foot, which can sometimes be done via the limited northern road systems. In remote areas, hasty checks can be made through set-downs by chartered float plane. More-thorough surveys are done from small portable camps that are moved every few days by helicopter or floatplane. Perhaps the most common survey method in the North is to cruise waterways and lakeshores by boat. Whatever the method, the logistics are similar to those for camping out. Results are often meagre, keeping the archaeologist constantly on the move, investigating several campsites and tool-flaking stations in a day. After a major site is found and evaluated, a crew may return to excavate for more remains.

The account that follows is based on my own experiences at Great Bear Lake in the Northwest Territories:

The life of an archaeologist is seasonal, as were the lives of the prehistoric peoples we study. Before the end of winter we have to complete plans for summer fieldwork, which involves hiring assistants, preparing equipment, determining local facilities and obtaining permits. We study the area to be surveyed by poring over topographical maps and air photographs and by reading explorers' accounts.

Then, one evening in June, we stand at the side of the gravel runway in the clear northern sunlight, sniffing the pungent fragrance of muskeg and shedding the urban civilization we left behind that morning, several flights ago. We make arrangements in the village for a boat rental, fuel and a local assistant, and within a few days the survey is under way. Discovery or disappointment or a measure of both is now at hand.

What we hope above all to find are large, rich, layered campsites that merit future excavation. But what we usually find are the skimpy remains of small family-size camps or hunter out-camps and a few widely scattered artifacts that may indicate a succession of camps established intermittently over a long period of time. Our survey is of the "judgemental" type, which focuses on the most likely and most accessible areas for ancient sites. We ignore bogs,

Plate 2. A Streambank Campsite
Located on a tributary of the Anderson River, northwest of Great Bear Lake, this is a typical late-prehistoric or early-historical fishing-camp site. The clearing may have been enlarged by its occupants. Depressions from levelled rectangular shelter-floors are near the edge of the bank, where fish scales from processing the catch are abundant in the soil. (Photograph by the author, CMC neg. 74-13617)

trackless forests, and expanses of terrain lacking features that might have attracted early inhabitants. Hunters did sometimes camp in such places, but it would be difficult to find and excavate the sites.

Cruising close to the lakeshore, we look for terraces and knolls, small peninsulas and ancient shoreline ridges that may once have made good campsites. We stop at all the stream mouths and narrows where there might have been fishing camps, and in small coves where early travellers might have put in for the night. We even check hilltops where lookouts might have spent the passing hours in making stone tools. We always inspect the exposed ground that nature provides—stream banks, sparsely vegetated places, and areas denuded by the wind. Sometimes we dig test pits in a likely location to see what is in the ground. Each day we stop many times to inspect these kinds of places; each night we make camp. Our technique has been perfected to the point that within a few minutes of pulling our boat into a protected spot, we have unloaded tents, sleeping bags and cooking gear, and have a pot of tea or coffee on the stove.

Through the summer we come across the remains of camps, tepee frames and caribou-hunting corrals from historical times. We find innumerable traces of ancient camps, often just fire-cracked rock where there had been a hearth. We dig up scattered, lost or broken stone tools and find terraces littered with stone chips from toolmaking. We see simple stone structures such as tepee rings, hearths and cache pits at ancient campsites. Where sufficient material is present we map the positions of the tools, features and stones.

Eventually it is time to leave the wilderness and return to the village, where we feel a little "bushy" from having seen so few other people. Before long, seated in the jet headed southwards, we replay in our minds the successes and failures of the summer. Our last leg of travel, on the morning business flight, reinforces our feeling that the Subarctic is indeed a different world, but undeserving of its popular image as a harsh, cold place.

Reading the Record

Surveys and excavations yield many different kinds of information. One kind comes in the form of artifacts and another from recovered trash, especially the bones of food animals and the waste left from toolmaking. Clues as to how people lived in the past can be derived from the number of tools found of each type, their association with other tools, how they are distributed around hearths or on dwelling floors, and the clustering of such features. Thus, both the features of excavations and the position of artifacts must be carefully recorded.

For analysis, the artifacts and information must be organized into distinctive groups of related materials. Style changes differentiating regions during the same period may indicate occupation by new tribes. But sequential changes occurring within a single area may represent stages in the development of a people's culture. Archaeologists have used a variety of terms to define and group related prehistoric remains. The most commonly used term is *phase*. Phases are usually local in distribution and of only a few centuries' duration. They mark minor differences. A series of phases linked in a sequence of development is termed a *tradition*, but traditions are often called *cultures*. Traditions are given names, and the component phases may be named or numbered. One tradition is likely to be interpreted as ending and another beginning when there have been major changes in tool styles and technology. This can occur through time as new people migrate into an area or when the local people undergo a very dramatic change. Widely separated peoples with different lifeways are also placed in different traditions. However, style boundaries are often not sharp. Subarctic traditions are usually defined on the basis of a few types of stone tools, so they tend to be primarily technological in nature. Their correlation with particular tribes is often highly uncertain. The influences that moulded past cultures have usually come from more than one source, and the interpretations of specialists accordingly may differ.

Various analytical techniques can be applied to archaeological finds. Dating of sites and artifacts is one means of establishing their chronology or sequence, and helps us to relate events with those in other areas. For purposes of interpretation, the relationships between artifacts, not just the artifacts themselves, are important. Their position on a dwelling floor, for example, may show that men and women had separate living areas, or may help to determine how many families occupied a dwelling. The appearance of exotic raw materials in implements and ornaments often indicates trade with outsiders. Trade routes or networks can be discovered by plotting the distribution of materials found in sites over a large area. That kind of information usually comes from studying the plentiful waste from stone chipping rather than the scarcer finished tools themselves. This is one reason why the archaeologist searches for prehistoric trash as diligently as for fine artifacts. Bone refuse identifies some of the game taken. And from that information one may be able to identify the seasons during which camps were occupied. However, the pitfalls of interpretation are many. For example, most northern peoples practised respectful disposal of animal remains, so what is recovered may not fully represent the animals actually hunted or eaten.

The characteristics or attributes of individual implements, such as spearheads, and of such features as shelter remains are singled out for analysis because style differences are useful indicators of change through time, or they may reflect regional differences and even tribal identity. Matching with similar items of known age helps to date an artifact, and is called *cross-dating*.

Most dating today is done in laboratories by the *radiocarbon-dating* method, which measures the trace amount of radioactive carbon-14 atoms in organic matter. The unstable 14-C isotope content begins to decrease at a known rate when an organism dies.

Plate 3. The Stratigraphy of an Excavation Wall Alternating layers of flood silt and soil lines mark 1 500 years of occupation at the Klo-kut site on the banks of the Porcupine River in the northern Yukon. The dark soil-bands often coincide with episodes of occupation. Burial by river silts has helped to preserve features and organic remains from disturbance and decay. (Photograph by Jacques Cinq-Mars, CMC neg. 71-4569)

Age is determined by applying this formula to the assay of residual radioactivity or to an actual count of 14-C atoms present.

In this book, dates calculated on the basis of the radiocarbon-dating method are rounded off to the nearest century, or to the half millennium where deemed appropriate. Researchers have found, through correlating these dates with tree rings, that radiocarbon dates of earlier than about 2 000 years ago tend to underestimate true age. The correction for dates of more than 8 500 radiocarbon years ago is only now becoming known. To dates between 8 500 and 5 000 years ago, the reader may wish to add about 800 years; to those between 5 000 and 2 000 years ago, add progressively less, down to zero correction.

Stopdates and *relative dates* are also useful. The date an old beach ridge was formed, for instance, provides a stopdate backwards that establishes the earliest possible date the ridge could have been occupied. When a location is occupied for a time, abandoned, and reoccupied, layered deposits (or strata) may be formed. The bottom layers will be older than the overlying layers. This stratigraphy accordingly provides relative dating. Natural events, especially *volcanic eruptions*, deposit distinctive layers marking a single moment in time; an example is the White River volcanic ash, to be treated in Chapter 3. Moreover, a single eruption can often be recognized and dated over a large area. Sometimes an implement has passed through gradual stylistic changes over its centuries of use. The sequence of these changes is determined through a process called *seriation*, which establishes a chronology against which new finds can be compared.

Many other dating methods exist, some of which have been used in the Western Subarctic. For example, obsidian (volcanic glass) has been dated, with mixed success, by measuring the thickness of an altered (hydrated) surface layer, seen only through microscopical examination of a thin section, and applying a time/rate formula that quantifies the growth rate of this layer. This is called *obsidian hydration dating*.

The study of prehistory is not limited to interpreting what comes out of the ground. Prehistorians also examine language distribution. For example, when two closely related dialects or languages are separated geographically, it can be inferred that a single speech community became split through migration or penetration by invaders. The creation of tree diagrams relating extant languages to one another is a standard technique for interpreting the framework of prehistory, but has had mixed success. It cannot identify speakers of extinct languages who vanished long ago, and whose traces exist only as archaeological records. Shared technologies or belief systems also reflect contacts between different peoples. Human biological traits and their distribution in the present provide evidence of the distribution and migration of racial groups in ancient times. Additional biological information comes from the study of human bones, though such studies are limited in the Subarctic by poor bone preservation and the reluctance of archaeologists to offend the sensitivities of indigenous peoples.

Archaeologists are also keenly interested in ancient geography because of its effects on human societies. They draw on the physical and natural sciences to learn about past climates, vegetation, wildlife and terrain. These conditions not only influenced past lifeways, but changes in the environment (as when lakes dried up and forests became grasslands) may account for some variations in the archaeological record that cannot otherwise be explained.

Explaining the Record

Archaeologists often appear to bury their subject under lengthy descriptions of artifacts, artifact styles and lists of culture traits. How can such a catalogue of data be made to reveal a history of human lives through ten thousand Subarctic years?

Artifacts can be interpreted within the framework of history, for example, through the succession of phases and cultures. But artifacts can also provide a picture of how people lived in ancient times. Every artifact and every site feature represents some person's interests, activities, individuality and abilities. But because of limitations in the data, the study of prehistory deals less with individuals than with groups. The group may be a band of Subarctic hunters and fishers or a cluster of bands that were very much alike culturally.

Culture is by definition the collective customs and technology of a group or a society, and the differences among them in these attributes are what give each group its distinctive identity. Thus, archaeologists seek to define phases and traditions in order to identify the tribes of prehistory and place them in time and space. To do so, they need to make intelligent guesses about the factors that resulted in cultural uniformity within Subarctic societies. For living models, archaeologists have turned to the Subarctic tribes of historical times.

According to the studies of ethnologists, Subarctic people came together in various kinds of settlements and social groups, ranging from independent nuclear families to settlements of freely associated hunting and fishing families, to bands led by a chosen leader. The loosely structured bands, with a fluid membership of probably one hundred persons, usually visited and intermarried with adjacent bands that spoke the same dialect. A cluster of bands interacting in this way might, in a very loose sense, be termed a *tribe*. But the tribes, too, had rather vague boundaries, where neighbouring bands of different tribes interacted socially and intergraded linguistically and culturally. The composition of tribes and bands was unstable They split up, merged or disappeared, and remnants of decimated groups were absorbed by others. Thus, political organization was extremely rudimentary in the Subarctic, but bands, and even the tribes within a relatively large area, generally shared the same cultural characteristics.

To return to the methodology of archaeology, the tendency for implements or styles to be standardized within an area allows prehistorians to define phases. The maintenance of commonalities in an area over a long period provides evidence of a distinct tradition. Interactions between people lead to the sharing of traits, while isolation results in divergence of development. There are, for instance, innumerable styles of arrow tips, but knowledge of a style must be transmitted by craftsmen to each new generation. In the North, most such interactions and training must have taken place within dispersed families and households, which came together at certain times each year in larger groups. Then the people had a chance to learn new things from one another or reinforce current ways. Thus, the distribution of technology and styles seen in Subarctic prehistory is thought to correlate with the organization and social interaction of the population. One has to be very cautious, however, in equating archaeological phases and traditions with tribal organization, since a tribe could be only very loosely defined in the Subarctic.

The settlements and camps of individual bands, households and hunting parties provide the only sound archaeological evidence, however fragmentary, of Subarctic social organization. Band members sometimes camped together at the same sites in a territory that supplied most of their subsistence requirements, but usually went farther afield when hunting big game. At certain times of the year local bands of several families worked and camped together, but most of the time people lived in isolated households of one or two families. Most of the archaeological sites represent the camps of these types of small social groupings. As noted earlier, the evidence at a site is often disturbed and hard to interpret, but close observation may yield useful information about social organization. For instance, if each hearth or dwelling floor at a site is clearly separated from the others, a large single-episode encampment of families can be inferred. On the other hand, if hearths and shelter traces randomly intersect, some disturbing others, consecutive smaller-scale episodes of camping can be visualized.

1. The Early Prehistory of the Northwestern Area
(11 500 to 7 000 Years Ago)

This chapter opens with an account of the Siberian origins of Canada's subarctic peoples, beginning with the late-Ice Age occupation of Beringia. The stage is set for succeeding events by descriptive accounts of the end of the Ice Age and the Palaeo-Indian occupation of the mid-continent. Narrowing our focus to the northwest, we will next discuss the settlement of lands newly freed from the ice. Almost concurrently, a new stone-tool technology and evidently a new people arrived from Asia. These microblade people are discussed in the last section of this chapter.

Siberian Roots

Expanding ice sheets eventually covered most of Canada during the Ice Age, from the Pacific to the Atlantic. With so much moisture locked up in ice, the sea level dropped, exposing a land connection with Asia in the area of Bering Strait. This vast treeless plain, which extended from the Yukon to eastern Siberia, is called Beringia. It was essentially isolated from the rest of North America by the converging western and eastern ice sheets, called the Cordilleran and Laurentide respectively, leaving Beringia as an appendage of Siberia. Thus, at this time, the peoples of eastern Siberia and the North American subarctic may have been branches of a single population.

Through earlier millennia, people had spread into southern Siberia, probably from Mongolia or China; later, by about 25 000 years ago, they reached the northeastern limits of Asia, and finally, at an undetermined date, arrived in North America. The harsh winters of the North necessitated protective clothing and shelters and the ability to track, stalk and kill game, virtually the only food source. By developing these skills, humans were able to occupy Siberia, to reach North America, and eventually to colonize the Western Hemisphere. Some stayed in the Subarctic, but others moved south, prospered, and developed complex civilizations.

One line of evidence bearing on the origins of Subarctic populations lies in the people themselves—in their slowly changing genetic code and its visible expressions, such as facial features, body build, and dentition. Generally speaking, Subarctic Indians are more Mongoloid in appearance than Plains Indians, but are less so than Eskimos. Given the widely accepted hypothesis that the arctic Mongoloid type (primarily Eskimos and northeastern Siberian peoples)

Map 3. Palaeo-Indian Migrations About 11 000–12 000 Years Ago

Ancestral Clovis people moved southwards between ice sheets either at this time or during some earlier era (longest arrow and branching front). Later some Clovis people turned north, colonizing land newly freed of ice (short north-pointing arrows). The arrow reaching only as far south as the Yukon and Alaska represents the microblade people about 11 000 years ago. This generalized migration pattern can also be applied to pre-Clovis migrations.

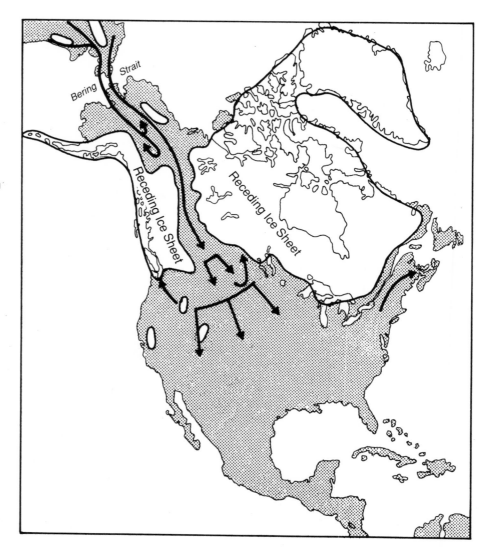

developed late in the history of human evolution, these differences are interpreted in terms of three migrations. Ancestors of the more southerly Indians came first, followed by the antecedents of the present Subarctic population, and about the same time by ancestral Eskimos. The differences they manifest may reflect genetic differences that existed earlier in their Asian homelands. However, some specialists propose that the intermediate physical appearance of Subarctic peoples is not due to a separate migration, but to a mixing of the ancestral Indian and Eskimo populations. Others support a third hypothesis, in which both Eskimos and northern Indians, especially Athapaskans, diverged from a formerly more-uniform population that inhabited Alaska at the end of the last Ice Age. In any case, subtle genetic characteristics, such as tooth attributes, indicate that all prehistoric migrations to the New World originated in northeastern Asia.

The Area

The region we refer to in this book as the Northwestern Area essentially lies west of the Mackenzie River and northwest of the Plains (Map 1). It includes not only part of the mountainous spine of North America, but also the lesser ranges extending to the Pacific coast and Arctic Ocean and the intervening uplands and river valleys. The region is extremely varied topographically and environmentally. Lowlands are often covered by a characteristic boreal forest dominated by spruce and liberally dotted with muskeg bogs, while the dry slopes where pine trees rise to prominence remind one of the sierra country of northern California. In the high country, there are vast open areas that provide easy travel routes.

Subarctic peoples live under some of the greatest temperature extremes on the continent. Enervating summer temperatures of 38°C occasionally occur, while at "cold sinks" (areas that trap cold air), virtually all activity ceases when the temperature remains day after winter day as low as minus 65°C. Over the entire Subarctic, winters are long, summers short, and spring and fall briefer still. Freeze-up and breakup are the major seasonal events. With freeze-up comes not only ice but snow, and eventually the advantage of moving about easily by sled, toboggan and snowshoe. But freeze-up can take several weeks, during which time preparations for winter will be

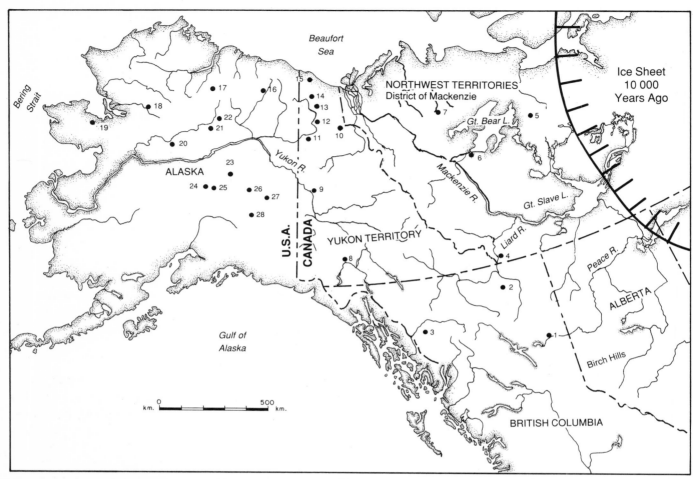

Map 4. Ancient Sites in the Northwestern Area, 11 500 to 7 000 Years Ago The sites shown belong to Clovis Palaeo-Indian, Palaeo-Arctic, and early Northern Cordilleran peoples. Microblade people of the Palaeo-Arctic tradition became established in Alaska around 10 700 years ago, and expanded eastwards, probably absorbing or displacing earlier inhabitants of the Cordilleran region.

1 Charlie Lake Cave, P-I	9 Dawson placer mines, P-I & Moosehide	19 Trail Creek Caves, P-A
2 Pink Mountain, P-I	10 Rock River sites, NC	20 Batza Téna, obsidian source, P-I
3 Mount Edziza, obsidian source	11 Bluefish Caves, P-I, P-A	21 Island, P-I, P-A
4 Fisherman Lake & Pointed Mountain, NC, P-A, HR	12 Old Crow River Flats, P-I	22 Girls' Hill, P-I
	13 Dog Creek, P-I	23 Campus, HR
5 Acasta Lake, NC	14 Kikavichik Ridge, P-I	24 Walker Road, P-I
6 Franklin Tanks, Gt. Bear R., HR	15 Engigstciack, NC, HR	25 Dry Creek, P-A
7 Airport, NC	16 Putu, P-I	26 Broken Mammoth, P-A, NC
8 Canyon Creek, NC	17 Mesa, NC	27 Healy Lake sites, NC, P-A
	18 Onion Portage, P-A, HR	28 Tangle Lakes, P-A

Abbreviations
P-I: Palaeo-Indian
P-A: Palaeo-Arctic
NC: Northern Cordilleran group
HR: Siginificant in history of research

completed. Breakup is part of the spring melt, and is also a season for waiting. Travel over any distance, by canoe or overland, is impossible until the thaw is well advanced.

The interiors of continents, including the Subarctic, are regions of low precipitation. Nevertheless, many years in the North have an inordinate amount of rain. This can have serious consequences in a region where survival depends upon being able to dry fish, prevent stored meat from spoiling, and keep skin clothing dry and pliable. Moreover, raw spring weather exacts a high death toll among caribou fawns and the young of other game animals, and poor catches result when fishing equipment has to be removed from swollen streams. Hardship on such a scale is the exception rather than the rule, but it occurs sporadically, and until relatively recently could decimate the population of a stricken area.

The Earliest Occupations

The earliest records of occupation in the Subarctic are from eastern Beringia, now interior Alaska–Yukon. Near the end of the Ice Age, glaciers still dominated parts of the mountainous northwest, but some intermontane areas were free of ice by 11 500 years ago, extending the open zone south and east of the former limits of Beringia. Late in the Ice Age and immediately after it, newly accessible areas of the northwest were settled from three directions: Beringia, the eastern foothills of the Rocky Mountains from Alberta to the Arctic Ocean, and the valleys and the interior Plateau of British Columbia. Erosion has destroyed or obscured most of the evidence. Nevertheless, we can connect the data from several distant points to create a coherent picture.

In northern North America, there are a few convincing traces of occupation earlier than 11 500 years ago. Thousands of semifossilized mammoth, bison, horse, caribou and other animal bones dated to an earlier era have been found in the Yukon, eroding from the banks of the Old Crow River. Some of the fractured and cut bones have been interpreted as butchered or intentionally worked, but all such bones had been transported there by soil creep and stream flow; a few stone tools were present, but their attribution to the earlier period is problematical. Moreover, no actual campsites have been found with which the seemingly modified bones can be associated.

Plate 4. Old Crow Flats An intensive search for "early man" has been conducted in the Porcupine River Valley and the adjoining Old Crow Basin, part of the Porcupine River drainage. (Night-time photograph by the author)

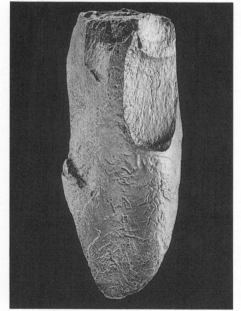

Plate 5. A Bone Flake from the Ice Age A fragment of a mammoth leg-bone, this 13-cm-long flake was recovered from a gravel bar in the Old Crow River, northern Yukon. Some archaeologists believe that it was intentionally struck off a larger piece of bone, perhaps for use as a tool.

Plate 6. The Bluefish Caves In the centre of the rock outcrop is the mouth of Cave 1. Hunters in the northern Yukon took temporary shelter in these small caves during the last ice age. The few tools and the chips from repairing tools that they left behind provide some of the earliest evidence of human occupation recovered in Canada. (Photograph courtesy of Jacques Cinq-Mars)

Plate 7. Bluefish Cave Artifacts Three burins (right), three microblades (top), and a microblade core and fragment at left (viewed from the top and side, respectively) were found in the Bluefish Caves. The burin at right is 5 cm long. (Photograph courtesy of Jacques Cinq-Mars)

They have been dated by the radiocarbon method to between 25 000 and 30 000 years ago, and in several cases earlier, but unfortunately there is no conclusive evidence that they have been modified by humans for use as implements.

A later but primary deposition site was found at the Bluefish Caves, located not far from the town of Old Crow. Two of the rock shelters sporadically provided refuge to hunters from about 20 000 to 10 000 years ago. Such occasional use has left only a sparse record, which includes fractured and apparently butchered bones; bone flakes; stone flakes (called burins) shaped in a specialized manner for use in carving and graving; small stone splinters, or spalls, derived from resharpening burins; and other stone tools, including a wedge-shaped microblade core and a few microblades. Microblades are also present among distinctive late-Ice Age tools found in Siberia. Successive deposit levels in the Bluefish Caves also yielded pollen grains, rodent bones and bones from several species of larger animals, all of which were analysed to determine what the environment was like when the deposits accumulated. The pollen indicates that changes occurred in the local vegetation, first from arctic tundra to shrubs and then, after the rock shelters largely ceased to be occupied, to spruce forest.

Indirect but controversial evidence of occupation before 12 000 years ago comes from regions far to the south, in the United States and South America. At times during the Ice Age the eastern and western ice sheets parted, leaving a corridor running north and south. Thus, people entering eastern Beringia from Asia would have had access to the entire Western Hemisphere. Numerous sites have been proposed as evidence of such migration, but the implements discovered there are not very distinctive and the validity of their proposed early dating has been questioned. A significant number of archaeologists demand more conclusive proof for the occupation of the Americas before 11 400 years ago.

That was the point in time when a distinctive technology, unequivocally establishing human occupation, began spreading across North America south of the ice sheets. This was the Clovis culture and its several regional variants, distinguished by lanceolate spear points with fluted or thinned bases. Clovis origins are a mystery. Many archaeologists suggest a period of development south of the ice sheets by Palaeo-Indians, who may have reached that part of the continent during an earlier migration from Siberia. On their way south, ancestral Palaeo-Indians must for a time have occupied the Western Subarctic, but their remains are so sparsely represented there that they cannot be positively identified. A less-favoured hypothesis is that fluted points were invented in Beringia and were carried southwards by migrants about 11 500 years ago, as the Ice Age was ending. While fluted points have been found in the Yukon and Alaska, their presence does not in itself prove that the Clovis culture originated there.

Big-game hunters were roaming eastern Beringia, that is, interior Alaska–Yukon, at the same time as Clovis people were spreading south of the wasting ice sheets. The next oldest evidence of northern occupation, after Bluefish, dates between 11 500 and 11 100 years ago. Stone tools of that period have been recovered primarily from campsites that lie buried within the soils, and are not isolated or surface finds. Spears were tipped with lanceolate points; other tools included teardrop-shaped and leaf-shaped knife blades, numerous scrapers in several shapes, and what appear to be large, thick planing tools. For blanks, from which to make the smaller tools, rough blades or bladelike flakes were struck from blocks (cores) of various fine-grained stones. The best-defined and most reliably dated group of this material is called the Nenana complex (*complex* is roughly equivalent to *phase*) and comes from sites located just north of the Alaska Range. Hearths have been found at one Nenana complex site, where there is also a sharply delimited distribution of artifacts that suggests the circular floor of a shelter—probably a conical skin tent. Another find was an isolated antler tool, possibly a punch, which was recovered in a placer mine near Dawson and has been dated to 11 350 years ago. Given their similar age and general tool similarities, a common ancestor to both the Nenana complex and the Clovis Palaeo-Indians may eventually be recognized in the North.

As the Ice Age drew to a close, people had to adjust to rapidly changing conditions, and began to occupy newly available territories. To grasp the extent and significance of these profound environmental changes, let us first examine the events that were taking place all over the North.

The End of the Ice Age

Deglaciation

Deglaciation began about 14 500 years ago and was well under way 12 000 years ago. A warming climate and melting ice caps produced one of the most volatile periods of environmental change in the Northern Hemisphere. But deglaciation did not proceed uniformly, and there were local re-advances of the ice. In each area, the time clock of Canadian human history was set when the land became free of ice and was ready for colonization.

The end of the Ice Age produced an uninhabitable landscape of a kind not seen anywhere on earth today. Its major feature is a dirt-strewn, rotting ice sheet enveloping all of Canada north and east of the ice-free central plains. Rills of meltwater slip across the surface to plunge into crevasses. Streams laden with glacial silt gush forth along the entire front of the ice sheet. In many places blocks of ice break off into the expansive meltwater lakes forming in the wake of the retreating ice. Glacial Lake McConnell, ancestor to both Great Bear and Great Slave lakes, has inundated northern Alberta. Its bare shores consist of ring after ring of rocky beach ridges marking former water levels; these levels fall drastically over the decades as new outlets open behind the receding ice sheet. West of Lake McConnell, in the Mackenzie River valley, the land is shrubby and seemingly hospitable, probably with poplar trees lining the watercourses. Great silty rivers flow through the valleys of the northwest and across the expanding mid-continental plains, carrying loads of glacial gravel and often changing course as channels become loaded with sediment.

Far to the northwest the sea gradually drowns the Bering Land Bridge, which had already been severed by 14 000 years ago. As the withdrawal of water into ice caps had lowered sea levels and created a connection between the continents, so the release of water by the melting ice was now resubmerging it.

The people who lived during the Ice Age and its aftermath had to contend with vastly different conditions than those encountered by their descendants 8 500 to 7 000 years ago. By 8 500 years ago nothing remained of the ice caps of western Canada, except in the northeastern corner of the Keewatin District. Many of the great glacial lakes had drained or assumed the forms of today's major lakes. However, Lake Agassiz, of which Lake Winnipeg is a remnant, and Lake Ojibway were still blocked by glacial ice to the north and had flooded an immense expanse of the Subarctic, from Saskatchewan to Quebec. The great weight of the ice caps had depressed the crust of the earth so much that, until the land rebounded, shallow seas covered much of today's northern lowlands. Between 8 000 and 7 000 years ago, the postglacial adjustments continued. The Hudson Bay Lowlands in northern Manitoba, Ontario and Quebec were still flooded by ancestral Hudson Bay, then part of the Tyrrell Sea.

The March of the Vegetation Zones

By 8 000 years ago, or earlier in some parts of the North, the climate had become warmer than it is now, prompting the rapid northward spread of the coniferous boreal forest into territory where there had been only ice and tundra. The early boreal forest was mainly spruce, but other species appeared later, to form a mixed forest. In time there were other changes, such as the development of muskeg bogs. Gradually, the land was revegetated. During the warm period that came soon after the glaciers melted, forests extended farther north than they do today, reaching the Arctic Ocean at the mouth of the Mackenzie River.

At the same time, farther south, the grasslands were spreading northwards at the expense of the forest. In Saskatchewan, for example, between about 8 500 and 4 700 years ago, during the warmest period, southern grasslands extended 170 kilometres farther north than they do today. Similarly, the boreal forest extended as much as 350 kilometres north of its present limit, into what are now the Barren Lands of the Northwest Territories. There is a close correlation between vegetation and animal life. Bison, for instance, thrive on grasslands, and caribou on the lichens of forest and tundra. Thus, the bison-hunting Plains Indians and the caribou-hunting peoples of the Subarctic must have followed the animals on which they depended northwards, and returned southwards as the climate subsequently cooled.

A Hunter's Paradise Lost

The end of the Ice Age was a period of species extinctions—of mammoths, mastodons, horses, lions and other mammals. Some species disappeared in North America only, while the same or closely related species survived in other parts of the world. As well, the ranges of surviving species sometimes changed. Though giant and super bison had disappeared, modern-type bison evolved and thrived, not only on the Plains but also in the Subarctic, where they were hunted by the people described later in this chapter. Muskoxen, which once roamed temperate lands south of the ice caps, also disappeared from that region, but one species continued to be a staple resource for more-northerly subarctic and arctic peoples. Other large Ice Age mammals hunted by the earliest inhabitants of Beringia included horse and caribou, and possibly mammoth and sheep. By 10 000 years ago, the inhabitants of the northwest (including the Palaeo-Arctic, Northern Cordilleran and Plano people described here and later) depended mainly on the barren-ground caribou. In some localities, however, woodland caribou, bison, moose, elk, sheep and muskoxen were important.

Postglacial environmental change appears to have been the main cause of the extinctions, although hunting by humans was a factor. Species competition for graze and browse increased as steppe tundra changed to shrub tundra and grasslands were broken up by advancing postglacial forests. These changes did not occur simultaneously, and are still going on. An example is the marked reduction of bison, which have been virtually eliminated in the Subarctic, but which just a few thousand years ago roamed the Yukon and adjacent territories.

Southern Palaeo-Indians in Subarctic Prehistory

As the glaciers retreated, the zone suitable for human occupation widened across southern Canada. Clovis spear points and related fluted projectile tips have been found over much of Canada south of the limits to which the glaciers and meltwater lakes had receded about 11 000 years ago. Evidently, hunters using fluted points occupied the new lands within a few centuries after the ice sheets had melted back.

Among the traces of Clovis culture that link the Palaeo-Indian prehistory of the Western Subarctic with that of the Plains are a number of spear points found between Edmonton and the Birch Hills of western Alberta. These surface finds cannot be dated, but a fluted point

Plate 8. Fluted Points The fragment, 2.8 cm long, is from the northern Yukon, and the obsidian point of the same length is from Alaska. (The latter was coated black for photography by the author.)

excavated from Charlie Lake Cave in northern British Columbia has been dated to 10 400 years ago. At that time it was impossible to penetrate to the heart of the Subarctic, for nothing but seas of meltwater and ice lay northeast of the Birch Hills and Charlie Lake, though there were open avenues extending to the northwest. Perhaps these fluted points are among the last of their kind, since point styles had changed by about 10 000 years ago. Big-game animals such as mammoths and mastodons were gone. People probably followed a seasonal pattern of bison hunting, supplemented by other hunting and gathering activities; this was a postglacial adaptation that had proved successful on the Plains.

Fluted-point people also lived farther north, in Alaska and the Yukon. Evidently, late-fluted-point people continued migrating northwards into the valleys of the Yukon and then turned west, spreading throughout northern and interior Alaska as far as Bering Strait. At first they found themselves in previously unoccupied land, but soon they encountered unrelated people expanding east and south from the interior region of Alaska and the Yukon that we now call Beringia. There must have been interaction between these ethnically, linguistically and culturally diverse northerners.

Point styles had changed by about 10 400 years ago (or a few centuries later in some areas) to other lanceolate varieties. The later point styles and the prehistoric cultures they are associated with are called *Plano*. Plano people subsequently occupied parts of the Subarctic lying north of the Plains as well as areas of eastern Canada that had been inaccessible to Clovis people.

In addition to adjusting to postglacial changes in resources, there were further adaptations for the Plano successors of Clovis to make. One Plano adaptation, beginning about 8 000 years ago, was to conditions in the North-Central Subarctic forests and on the frontier of the Barren Lands, as described in Chapter 5. To the west, there were other people in the uplands and valleys of the Rocky Mountain region of northern British Columbia, the Yukon, and the western District of Mackenzie. As has been suggested of the Plano, these northwesterners may be descended from the fluted-point people. But it is equally plausible, on the basis of the limited information available at present, that their ancestors were the ancient Beringians (including the Nenana-complex people) who occupied the subarctic zone of the

Plate 9. Artifacts of Early Non-Micro-blade Cultures These artifacts, which are between 7 000 and 11 000 years old, were left by peoples who lived in the northwest before the Palaeo-Arctic microblade people arrived, or were contemporaries who had a different technology. The biface knife, small stone wedge and projectile tip at lower right are from the deepest levels of the Healy Lake site in eastern Alaska; the spearhead at top right, which is 8.2 cm long, is from the earliest occupation of the Canyon site in the southern Yukon; the Kamut-style spearhead and knife blade at top left, estimated to be between 5 000 and 8 000 years old, are from the Rock River in the northern Yukon; two projectile points, a burin and a drilled-pebble pendant in the middle row, from the Firth River in the northern Yukon, represent the Flint Creek complex. The apparently early knife and point at lower left come from Fisherman Lake in the southwestern Mackenzie District.

mountainous west. To facilitate discussion, we will refer to these north-westerners as the Northern Cordilleran group.

Northern Cordilleran Prehistory

The eastward expansion of the Northern Cordilleran group and the northward migration of fluted-point makers must have resulted in encounters, in the vicinity of the Mackenzie River valley, of two long-separated peoples who had developed different languages and lifeways. The complexity of these events may account for the complexity of the archaeological record, and has led to the development of hypotheses that have not yet been substantiated by field data.

Important finds were made in northernmost Yukon. These finds, termed the Flint Creek phase, are from a location where migrating caribou now cross the Firth River, less than 20 kilometres from the Arctic Ocean. The original excavations, done many years ago, re-covered several lanceolate spear points, perforators (or gravers), burins, knives, endscrapers, heavy chopping implements, and small pendants of red-shale pebbles. Among the animals eaten by Flint Creekers were bison, caribou, hare and birds. Radiocarbon dating of refuse bones shows that the Flint Creek phase began nearly 10 000 years ago, but we cannot be certain that all the finds are of this age. Some may be appreciably later. No hearths or shelter floors were uncovered, so we only know these people by a few of their tools, faunal refuse, and the circumstantial evidence for big-game hunting afforded by the site location.

In a very different setting, 850 kilometres away in the southern Yukon, a small family, or perhaps a hunter and his partner, stopped at Canyon Creek after an apparently successful bison hunt in a valley east of Kluane Lake. They built a fire, stayed a little while, and then moved on, but not before they had replaced a broken spear point, flaked some other tools, and lost a very well-made round-based spear point. When archaeologists found the site on a bluff above the Aishihik River, it was buried under two metres of wind-blown sand. They obtained a radiocarbon date of 7 200 years ago from charcoal remaining in the patch of reddened earth where the campfire had once blazed. The vegetation in the region at that time was mixed grassland and forest.

Campsites at Fisherman Lake, located far to the east of Canyon Creek, at the edge of the mountains in the southwestern District of Mackenzie, were first settled as early as 8 500 years ago. The evidence includes leaf-shaped and stemmed points as well as scrapers and knives. The people who made these tools might have been Plano colonists from the northern plains, but it is more likely that their ancestors had already had a long history of development in the North along the eastern edge of the Rocky Mountains.

People related to the Northern Cordilleran group also spread into the northern part of the Mackenzie District. Their tools, collectively termed the Acasta phase, were found in campsites east of Great Bear Lake, and date back to 7 000 years ago. Because of their easterly location, the people of Acasta Lake are described in Chapter 5, which deals with the North-Central Area.

Several sites of similar age and characteristics in interior Alaska, including the Mesa site, can be linked with those in northwestern Canada. The people who occupied these camps 10 000 to 7 000 years ago are distinguished primarily by their lanceolate spear points and elongate stone knives. They shared part of the region with the Early Palaeo-Arctic microblade people, but, to anticipate the story told in the next chapter, the use of microblade tools had declined by 7 000 years ago and continued in only a few areas. Evidently, Northern Cordilleran people, who did not use microblade tools, had been prospering and expanding. Whether they replaced Palaeo-Arctic people or simply influenced them to drop microblades in favour of other types of tools is not known.

Microblade Technology in the New World

When strictly defined, the term *microblades* refers to a stone-tool technology. Technology can spread through migration of the users or through the process of cultural borrowing. Thus, the appearance of microblades in an area could indicate either the arrival of new people or the adoption of a new technology from neighbours. The use of microblades was not limited to one subarctic racial, linguistic or ethnic group. The North American distribution is connected with a broader Siberian and Asian distribution, pointing to ancient contacts between continents. In North America, microblades were used

Plate 10. Microblade Technology
Early toolmakers detached thin, sharp microblades from specially prepared blocks of stone, or "cores," in the manner depicted here. The microblades were trimmed at one end or both, and inserted into bone or wooden hafts to serve as cutting tools. Such composite tools required less stone than a large biface knife blade.

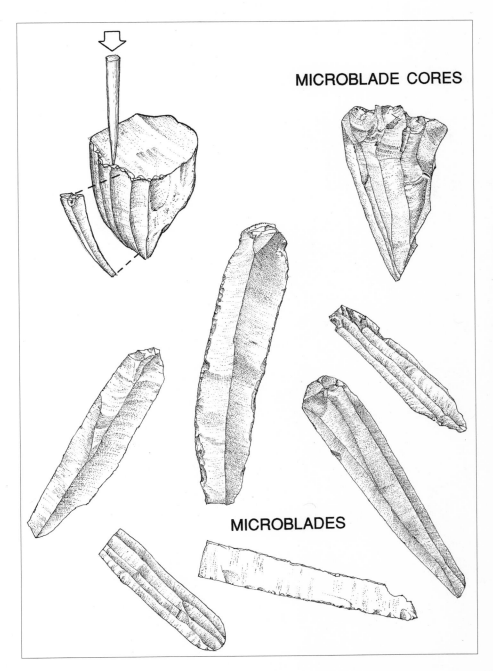

MICROBLADE CORES

MICROBLADES

primarily in the northwest. Even those found in the Eastern Arctic are linked to Palaeo-Eskimo migration from the west.

Some time after they became known in Asia, microblades appeared in western Alaska, and gradually spread eastwards to the Mackenzie River valley and to tributaries like the Athabasca River. Their first appearance in Alaska actually predates some of the sites or cultures already discussed here, whereas in other areas they were not present until later.

Manufacture and Use of Microblades

Microblades are regularly shaped, tiny, elongate, straight-sided, flat stone flakes. They can be compared with injector- razor and scalpel blades in terms of size, shape, sharpness and use. It takes specialized stone-knapping skills to produce them. Ironically, although countless thousands have been found, we know little about their use. We do know that some were inserted into grooved bone or antler spearheads to make vicious cutting edges that would hasten bleeding. Others were hafted for use as small cutting tools. It would be incautious to overstress the importance of a single type of tool, but learning to make and use microblades is a particularly complex process. The stone cores from which microblades are detached have to be prepared, and if the core contains a flaw there are procedures for correcting it. Most implements fitted with microblades required thin cutting edges, thus necessitating the creation of special slotted handles. Finally, the skills needed to use delicately edged microblade tools would have differed from those required by an ordinary flint knife. Acquiring new skills may require careful instruction to change deep-seated motor habits. For reasons like these, archaeologists attribute great importance to microblades.

Out of Asia, into Alaska and Canada

Microblade people appeared in Alaska from Asia soon after the end of the Ice Age. They camped at Dry Creek, in the centre of the state, 10 700 years ago. They were present farther east in the Tanana drainage, just west of the Yukon border, some time between 10 500 and 10 000 years ago. Most evidence for the presence of microblade people farther east—in the Yukon, the western Mackenzie District, and northern interior British Columbia—is later. Strictly considered, it

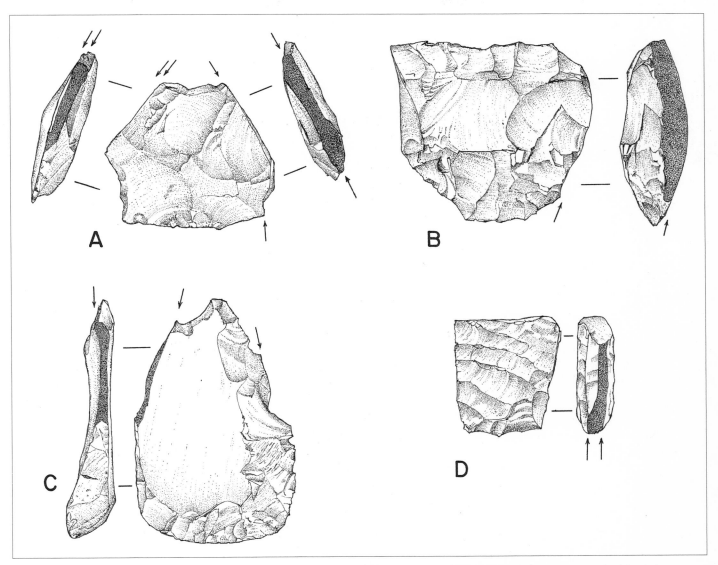

Plate 11. Burin Technology Burins are tools with edges formed by a peculiar technique, often associated with early cultures. With one deft stroke—the "burin blow"—the toolmaker created a cleft surface, or burin facet, indicated here by the darkened edges. The arrows indicate the direction of the burin blows, and point to the burin facets. In the diagram, four burins are shown in both full-face and edge views. A and B are transverse burins, C is an endscraper with two burin facets, and D is a burin made from the base of a broken spear point. The burins were shaped for their intended use, as either a carving bit, a groover or a scraping tool.

remains to be proved that the Palaeo-Arctic (ancient Arctic) people actually migrated from Siberia to Alaska. Possibly, the microblade technique was adopted by some Northern Cordilleran people who learned about it from Siberians just across Bering Strait. Inasmuch as the Beringian land connection with Siberia had been severed some three thousand years earlier, the free flow of people and ideas between Asia and North America was probably limited to communities on either side of Bering Strait. It is reasonable to conclude, therefore, that the successful establishment of Palaeo-Arctic, that is microblade, technology in eastern Beringia was attributable to immigrant bands. Subsequently, the technology could have spread through diffusion and migration. However, few Northern Cordilleran people used microblades. Maintainance of this technological cleavage through several millennia suggests that separate people and languages were present within the North.

Mainly stone Palaeo-Arctic implements have been recovered. They include leaf-shaped and lanceolate points often used as knife blades; large, broad knife blades; endscrapers; and simple but specialized carving, graving and scraping tools called burins. Microblades were struck from wedge-shaped cores. This core form persisted for several thousand years and is traced to the Diuktai culture of eastern Siberia. Simpler blocky and roughly conical-to-cylindrical microblade cores were also used in the North, especially by later peoples. These cores have later counterparts in Siberia, possibly indicating continued influence from Asia, or they may have been developed locally. There are also blades, which are the larger, more irregular, less numerous equivalent of microblades. Blades were often shaped into various tools.

Fluted points have been found with microblades in a few sites. They may be evidence of contact between Clovis-derived fluted-point hunters and Palaeo-Arctic people, who originally lived thousands of kilometres apart. But to what extent these peoples mingled and interacted remains to be determined.

From 10 000 to 8 000 years ago, one branch of Palaeo-Arctic people developed maritime fishing and sea-mammal hunting techniques in southwestern Alaska, and colonized the previously uninhabited shores and islands along the western coast of British Columbia and Alaska. About 1 000 or 1 500 years later, microblades appeared in the Plateau region of central British Columbia. Regional differences occurring in microblade-core varieties and associated implements, together with the great extent of the territories occupied, probably indicate that the microblade users of the Subarctic and the Plateau regions were different tribes and spoke different languages. At least 9 000 years ago, coastal people were getting obsidian from the interior for stone tools, including microblades. One source was Mount Edziza, located near the Stikine River in northern British Columbia. Barring the unlikely explanation that coastal people made expeditions to the source, or that the coast and the interior were occupied by the same people, there must have been trade at a very early time between the peoples of the Subarctic and the Pacific Coast.

Palaeo-Arctic people were in a position to reach the Yukon about 10 000 years ago, but, as is described in the next chapter, they seem to have been tardy, the hunters of the Bluefish Caves in the northern Yukon excepted. This region was already occupied by Northern Cordilleran groups, who may have remained uninfluenced by the microblade people. After about 8 000 years ago the use of microblades was declining, possibly in the face of the spread of Northern Cordilleran people.

Lifeways

Interpretation of the evidence bearing on early-prehistoric lifeways is inferential, based on site location and on the food resources and hunting technology of the times. What we know of the annual cycle of subsistence activities followed by historical Subarctic populations may not be applicable to the earliest prehistoric times. Nevertheless, in assessing the intelligence and ingenuity of northern peoples, there are no grounds for assuming that they were any different 11 000 years ago than 1 000 years ago. They had probably devised fish traps and game corrals, knew how to make snowshoes, build canoes and a variety of shelters, and could secure food caches from marauding animals. There is no conclusive evidence, however, that the bow and arrow was known. Food refuse bones recovered from the early sites are so sparse that in many instances they could be misleading. Most past environments were probably not very different than those prevailing in the North today. But the distribution of tundra, forest and bog in each locality was probably different than it is today, and this would have affected the availability of game locally and perhaps regionally.

2. The Middle Era of Northwestern Prehistory
(7 000 to 1 300 Years Ago)

We now turn to the events that took place during the next several thousand years, beginning about 6 000 or 7 000 years ago. Thus far, we have seen that near the end of the Ice Age there were people living in ice-free Beringia. Later, as the Ice Age ended and the glaciers retreated, the mountainous west was colonized from the south by Late Palaeo-Indians, and from the northwest by Northern Cordilleran descendants of the ancient Beringians. Earlier, about 10 700 years ago, Palaeo-Arctic people possessing a microblade technology had reached Alaska from Siberia. As lands farther east were freed of glacial ice and the immense meltwater lakes drained into the sea, the very late Palaeo-Indian people, called Plano, moved northwards into the North-Central Area of the Canadian Subarctic.

Some of these peoples prospered, but the Palaeo-Arctic tradition—representing many peoples who used microblade and burin technology—was displaced from parts of the northwestern interior. Elsewhere, the tradition changed considerably through the adoption of tools or implement styles from neighbouring groups.

The Northern Cordilleran people, whose beginnings were described in Chapter 1, supplanted or absorbed the Palaeo-Arctic people in some areas. As the use of microblade tools began to decline in the far-western Subarctic about 7 000 or 8 000 years ago, people adopted Cordilleran-style flaked spearheads for their weapons. We cannot be sure if this represents only a change in technology, or if it signals the replacement of many Palaeo-Arctic groups by Northern Cordilleran bands. Nevertheless, as noted in the previous chapter, some Late Palaeo-Arctic people not only survived but migrated eastwards into the southern Yukon, across northern British Columbia, and into northern Alberta and the District of Mackenzie. This chapter outlines the final eastward spread of Late Palaeo-Arctic people and their encounter with a new culture, the Northern Archaic.

Late Palaeo-Arctic People of the Yukon

Late Palaeo-Arctic people arrived in the southern Yukon, probably from Alaska, some 6 000 years ago, or slightly earlier. Microblades and the wedge-shaped cores from which they were struck continued to characterize the Late Palaeo-Arctic. Other implements included burins, leaf-shaped and stemmed spearheads, pointed knives, and various forms of scrapers. Few of the large blunt-ended biface knives

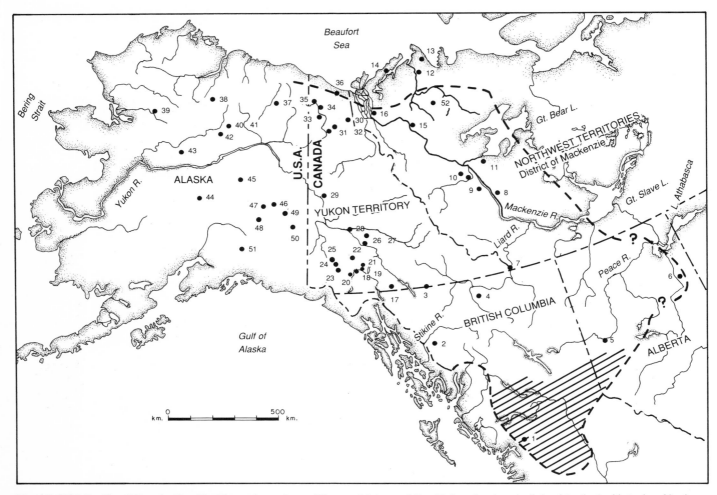

Map 5. Middle-Era Sites in the Northwestern Area The prehistory of the Yukon is closely linked to that of interior Alaska, some of whose main sites are included on this map.

1 Anahim Peak, Rainbow Range, obsidian source
2 Mount Edziza, obsidian source
3 Callison, NA
4 Muncho Lake, M
5 Karpinsky (Taltheilei?)
6 Bezya, M
7 Fisherman Lake & Pointed Mountain, M, NA, LP
8 Esker Bay, M, NA, LP
9 Drum Lake, M, LP
10 Yellow & Stewart lakes sites, fused-tuff source

11 Franklin Tanks & Great Bear River, NA, P-E
12 Anderson River, fused-rock source
13 Bathurst Peninsula ("Burning Cliff"), fused-rock source
14 NkTj-1, NA
15 Chick Lake, P-E
16 Whirl Lake, LP
17 Annie Lake, NA
18 Champagne
19 Taye Lake, NA
20 Canyon Creek, M, NA
21 Otter Falls, M

22 Chimi, M, NA
23 Airdrop Lake site, Hoodoo Mountain, obsidian source
24 Gladstone, NA
25 Little Arm, M
26 KbTx-2, M
27 Tatlmain Lake, LP
28 Pelly Farm, NA
29 Moosehide, M, NA, LP
30 Rock River, Late NC, NA
31 Old Chief Creek, NA, LP
32 Rat Indian Creek, NA, LP
33 Trout Lake, NC, P-E
34 Old John Lake, M, NA

35 Anaktuvuk Pass, NA, P-E, LP
36 Onion Portage, NA-type site, P-E, LP
37 Cathedral Mountain, unique
38 Girls' Hill, M, NA
39 Island, NA
40 Batza Téna, obsidian source, NA
41 Minchumina Lake, NA, LP
42 Campus, M or NA
43 Healy Lake sites, M, NA, LP
44 Donnelly Ridge, M

(continued from p.44)

Abbreviations
NA: Northern Archaic and/or Hybrid
M: Microblade (Late Palaeo-Arctic)
P-E: Palaeo-Eskimo
LP: Late prehistoric

Plate 12. Distinctive Artifacts of the Microblade People The four blade tools in the middle row, the microblades in the bottom row, and the five microblade cores scattered throughout characterize the microblade people. The spear point in the top row is from the Campus site in Alaska, where this technological tradition was first recognized in North America. The longest blade (centre) is 7.5 cm long.

45

that characterize most other Subarctic peoples have been found. As recovery of Palaeo-Arctic artifacts is limited to stone implements, we are left with a biased and incomplete picture of the Palaeo-Arctic people.

Like others who subsequently lived in the area, they undoubtedly used all available fish and game resources, ranging from ground squirrels to bison. Fishing was important seasonally, and large autumn catches could be stored for winter use. Mountain sheep were a highly esteemed food.

By 4 000 years ago, Palaeo-Arctic peoples had disappeared from the Yukon, adjacent northern British Columbia, and southern Alaska. Cultural succession took several forms. In certain areas, for instance, the Palaeo-Arctic microblade peoples had been replaced by the Northern Cordilleran lanceolate-point peoples, who subsequently developed the Northern Archaic culture, a new culture described below. Elsewhere, the succession was also largely technological; a hybrid technology was created when Northern Archaic tools, including notched points, were combined with the tools of the microblade people. This hybrid, which seems to have been the product of two forces—continuity with the past and external influence—had sufficient vitality to persist for several thousand years. Archaeologists have described it under various names, including the Late Denali phase and the Northwest Microblade tradition, and as a variant of the Northern Archaic.

A pure Palaeo-Arctic culture persisted in a few places, but it was finally replaced about 4 500 to 4 000 years ago by the Northern Archaic technology or by a hybrid type. The microblade hybrid continued to exist until A.D. 100 or later in a few areas. Just what these tool and implement changes signify in terms of events and tribal relationships may vary in different localities. In the southern Yukon, for example, one group of people probably supplanted another, but the Late Palaeo-Arctic people did not necessarily become extinct biologically. Elsewhere, under the influence of their neighbours, some adopted Northern Archaic technology. As described in Chapter 3, the Northern Archaic people themselves gradually changed over time; their descendants are today's Athapaskan Indians.

Plate 13. Late Palaeo-Arctic Tools from the Southwestern Yukon In the bottom row, from the left, are three transverse burins and another burin type; in the middle row, two end-scrapers and two gravers; and in the top row, a leaf-shaped knife or spear-head 7.3 cm long, a fine uniface blade, and the base of a projectile point of a style that is suggestive of earlier fluted points.

Palaeo-Arctic Migrations

While the Northern Archaic culture was developing, microblades not only remained in use in certain areas but continued to spread eastwards as far as the Athabasca River in Alberta. Migrating bands of Palaeo-Arctic people may have been responsible, but technology can also spread through the transmission of knowledge from one group to another, even among tribes that speak different languages. In fact, the diverse styles of stone implements and tool kits found with microblades in different areas suggest that learning from neighbours was a more significant force for change than migration. Regional differences notwithstanding, there were many similarities in technology across the Western Subarctic, indicating that there were contacts between peoples, sometimes face-to-face and sometimes indirectly through intermediate groups.

The evidence indicates that Palaeo-Arctic people actually settled in the southwestern Mackenzie District, probably displacing Northern Cordilleran people. On the other hand, the scattered pattern of microblades found in northern Alberta indicates that they may have been left by a few very mobile bands of Late Palaeo-Arctic people who made occasional journeys into the province. For most of the Mackenzie Valley region, the impetus for the adoption of microblades probably came from the far west. Mackenzie Valley tribes were also influenced by neighbours to the south and east, though they should be seen as a distinct Subarctic entity.

The Northern Archaic Culture

From a continent-wide perspective, the term *Archaic stage* refers to a hunting-gathering adaptation to modern environments following the Ice Age and preceding the development of native agriculture. The distinction this term conveys as a stage of cultural and historical development is much less cogent when applied to Canada's Subarctic, where no form of agriculture, even animal husbandry, was ever developed.

Beginning 6 000 to 5 000 years ago, depending on the area, large side-notched points—characteristic of Archaic tools—were adopted across the entire Subarctic. The notching of spear points to improve hafting evidently originated far to the south, since this trait is oldest on the Plains and in eastern North America. Nevertheless, there is little other evidence of contacts between the subarctic and temperate regions that would account for northern acquisition of Archaic-style notched points. East of Lake Athabasca and Great Slave Lake, side-notched points mark the beginning of the Shield tradition (Chapter 5). The cultures of the Mackenzie River basin display a blend of western, Plains and local developments. West of the Mackenzie River, side-notched points herald the emergence of the Northern Archaic tradition—an aggregation of diverse local groups—though such points are also present in the hybrid microblade culture. The Northern Archaic appears to be basically a western tradition that developed primarily out of local Northern Cordilleran antecedents and to some degree also from the Palaeo-Arctic culture.

Early Developments

Six thousand years ago, Northern Archaic bands roamed northern Alaska and the northern Yukon. Considering the apparent southern origin of Northern Archaic notched points, the initial development of this tradition probably occurred in the Cordillera of northern British Columbia nearly 7 000 years ago. But, ironically, the oldest identified finds come from northern Alaska. Apparently, Northern Archaic people actually replaced the previous inhabitants in some areas only. In most places, the indigenous population simply adopted side-notched points along with other new traits. Distributed through a range of local cultures, these traits together distinguish the Northern Archaic tradition. By 5 000 years ago, the Northern Archaic had spread to nearly every part of Alaska, but the southern Yukon remained a Late Palaeo-Arctic pocket for another 500 years. Because the Northern Archaic tradition did not arise from a single local ancestor, it did not interfere with continued local diversity nor the development of the hybrid microblade culture.

Until suitable information is obtained in the northern Yukon, we have to turn to northwestern Alaska for a description of the early Northern Archaic tradition where it was first defined—the Onion Portage site on the Kobuk River. There, people constructed their shelters, lit their hearth fires, and pursued the routines of life from about 6 000 to 4 200 years ago. Then they were abruptly extirpated from the site by Palaeo-Eskimos, but continued to occupy interior reaches of the country. Implements they lost at their riverside camp were buried under flood silts. These include side-notched spear points and other styles of points; very numerous, simply prepared end-scraper blades; broad side-hafted semilunar knives and pointed, butt-hafted, dagger-shaped knives; slate bars used as whetstones; choppers made from selected flat river-cobbles notched for hafting; and plain notched pebbles that may have been net sinkers. Burins and microblades were not in use as they had been in Palaeo-Arctic times.

The Northern Archaic in the Yukon

Northern Archaic people entered the southern Yukon about 4 500 years ago. The assumption that they were newcomers rather than descendants of the previous inhabitants, the Palaeo-Arctic, is reinforced by the magnitude of the differences between the two cultures. Northern Archaic camp remains became numerous about 3 000 years ago. They were of the Taye Lake phase, one of the local variants of this tradition. At the same time, people of the Old Chief Creek phase lived in the northern Yukon. As there are many similarities between the two, we will present a composite picture based on both.

Sites were now large. Evidently people reoccupied favourable locations seasonally over many generations. No dwelling remains have been found in the southern Yukon, save a possible tent ring, but they have been found farther north, where semisubterranean houses first appeared. One housepit at the Old Chief Creek site measured about 6 by 8 metres. The floor was dug 45 centimetres below ground level, but the surrounding berm of dirt dug from the pit increased the effective depth to about 65 centimetres. This is a very large dwelling for the Subarctic, and other Old Chief houses are smaller. They date relatively late in the Northern Archaic, to 2 000 years ago. These houses were probably low, roofed with poles, and covered with turf for insulation. There were no windows, but the smoke-hole served as a skylight. Unfortunately, few implements were left in the abandoned Old Chief Creek houses.

No such houses were built in the southern Yukon. There, and throughout most of subarctic Canada, dwellings were often portable, consisting of lean-tos, sheds, and various conical and domed

Plate 14. Northern Archaic Points
This selection of points, primarily from the Yukon, shows the variations in this common implement within the Northern Archaic tradition. The broadest specimen (bottom row), with its tip missing, is a knife blade; the others are spear points. The longest point (top left) is 12.5 cm long.

Plate 15. Heavy Northern Archaic Tools Notched cobbles like the one at bottom were used for net weights and hammerheads; this specimen is 16.6 cm long. Others have a prepared chopping edge, as in the wide specimen from Alaska at top right. The third item has been carefully shaped by flaking, perhaps to make a heavy scraping or chopping tool. Tools of this kind are common in the Yukon, northern British Columbia, and Alaska.

Plate 16. Bone and Antler Tools
Objects of these materials are rarely preserved in the Subarctic except at relatively recent sites. Two older items from the southern Yukon, dating from about 3 000 years ago, include an antler hammer and a barbed prong, 12.5 cm long, from a leister, or fish spear.

shelters, often covered with hides. These have left few traces other than hearths and scattered artifacts on poorly defined floors.

People fished and hunted caribou, moose, small game, and bison. Northern Archaic times were not static. A warming trend caused spruce forests (which thrive in a cool, moist climate) to retreat, and improved the habitat for large game.

Northern Archaic technology differed in several respects from that of Palaeo-Arctic people. Most significantly, microblades are absent, as are burins. The notched spear points and the short notched knives are new. Other point styles, particularly lanceolate, were also produced. In many respects, the tools from these Yukon sites are like the older ones from the Onion Portage site in Alaska. The trimmed-slab hide-scraping stone, or *chitho*, appears, but not as frequently as it did later, when it became the most prevalent of all Athapaskan stone tools. Northern Archaic people used many large blunt-ended biface knives as well as thick scrapers of different shapes. A number of crude tools were made from broken cobbles, though they do not appear consistently at all sites. Also found in a few sites were side-notched and edge-battered cobble weights or sinkers, which are characteristic of the Northern Archaic elsewhere. Fragments of carved-bone points and tools suggest that, if ever a site with good organic preservation is discovered, we can expect to find bone and antler implements that would considerably enhance our knowledge and appreciation of the Northern Archaic culture.

The Hybrid Microblade Culture

Sites combining artifacts of both the Palaeo-Arctic and Northern Archaic traditions are very common in interior Alaska north of the Alaska Range, and extend as far east as Dawson in the Yukon. A separate cluster of sites with similar characteristics is located in the western Mackenzie District. The two branches may briefly have been one culture, also encompassing the Yukon. The Mackenzie branch later diverged from both its local antecedents and the Alaska branch. During its span of several thousand years, the hybrid tool kit underwent further change, suggesting that changes must have been occurring in other aspects of culture.

Several variations in the composition of tool kits were present in the region extending from the Mackenzie Delta to northern Alberta.

Plate 17. Tools from the Mackenzie River Valley The prismatically shaped blade (second from top left) may be a tool blank. On its right are two hook-shaped scrapers that are remarkably similar in style; yet one is from the north shore of Great Bear Lake, the other from the southwest corner of the Mackenzie District. The small tip between them was found in a microblade site at Great Bear Lake. The two glossy stemmed knives with angled edges (lower right), made of fused tuff from the low hills west of Fort Norman, were found near the outlet of Great Bear Lake. Also shown are three spearheads and, at bottom row centre three scrapers of different formats. The spearhead at bottom left is 9.8 cm long.

These differences can be attributed to several causes. For example, contacts with different neighbouring peoples would have been a source of variety and variation in the adoption of new ways. As was noted earlier in this chapter, the first appearance of microblades in the Mackenzie branch evidently originated in migration from the far west. These migrants could have acted as "kickers," stimulating wider adoption of microblade technology.

Among the places where remains have been found are Fisherman Lake and nearby Pointed Mountain in the southwest District of Mackenzie. The locality had been occupied almost continuously from 8 000 years ago, and probably earlier. From 4 000 (possibly 5 000) to 2 000 years ago, people here made and used microblades. Other artifacts from this period include leaf-shaped and notched spear points, and points with stems offset by square shoulders. There are burins, large thick scrapers, endscrapers, gravers, drills, and shaft smoothers, all made of stone. The less-durable bone or antler artifacts that must once have accompanied the stone tools decayed and disappeared into the acid soils long ago. The Northwest Microblade tradition is the pioneer term still used by some archaeologists for these remains and those of other sites of the hybrid microblade culture in the Yukon, northern British Columbia and western Mackenzie District. Many of these implements from the southwest Mackenzie District are similar to the older tools of the Palaeo-Arctic tradition; others suggest contacts between Plains Archaic and Northern Archaic peoples. As Fisherman Lake is located just north of the Plains, it is not surprising that contact occurred.

Far to the north, at Whirl Lake, located at the southern edge of the Mackenzie Delta, is another example of the hybrid microblade culture. It makes an interesting contrast with Pointed Mountain, as both sites represent mutually isolated local groups of microblade-using people. Stone artifacts from Whirl Lake include microblades, large blades, graver tips on blades, well-made short lanceolate and leaf-shaped projectile points, and various common scrapers. No burins were found, nor are there any notched points, but the collection is too small to say which implements the Whirl Lake tool kit lacked.

3. The Threshold of History in the Northwest
(1 300 Years Ago to European Contact)

The anonymity of prehistory can never be dispelled. Yet we must try to identify the peoples who "wrote" the successive chapters of Subarctic prehistory. That amounts to tracing the development of cultures back to their roots. For late-prehistoric material, this is usually done by attributing remains to the ancestors of the first-reported historical inhabitants of the region involved. There is a risk of error in this practice, because even indirect contact with Europeans in eastern North America resulted in some tribes being displaced westwards. With prudent interpretation of the archaeological evidence, however, historically based identifications can be carried back for many centuries. This approach is more successful at richer sites, where there is a range of stylistically distinct items that can be used to demonstrate continuity through time, but rarely is the evidence that solid in the Subarctic. Moreover, the relocation of many groups during the fur-trade period often makes the identification of prehistoric tribes uncertain.

The late period of prehistory described in the present chapter leads to the tribes encountered by the first European explorers and traders in the eighteenth and nineteenth centuries. Prehistorians are reluctant to identify specific tribes of earlier times, but they try to correlate archaeological material from all but the remotest periods with language families that form a cluster of tribes, the Athapaskans for instance. The Northern Archaic people discussed in the previous chapter, who lived in the southern Yukon, have been identified as early Athapaskan speakers. Athapaskan speech is thought to have diverged about 4 000 years ago from ancestral stock in the same area, including adjacent parts of Alaska and British Columbia. This does not mean, though, that all the Athapaskan Indians now distributed from northwestern Alaska south to Mexico necessarily arose from that source.

The identity of any other peoples who may once have lived and died in the northwestern Subarctic is not known. Their lineages and languages have died out within the region, leaving no modern representatives there.

The Northern Yukon: Precursors of the Kutchin
During spring, the Vunta, one of the widespread Kutchin-speaking Athapaskan groups, could be found camped at the Klo-kut, Old Chief

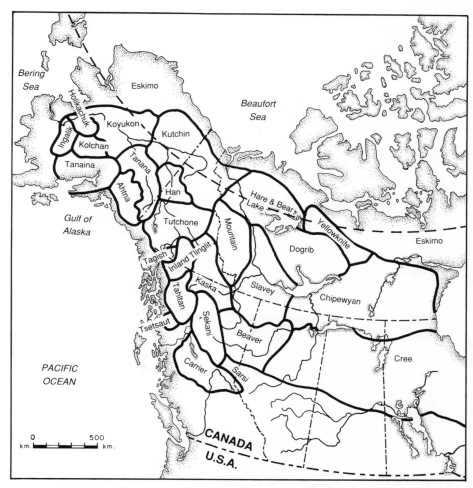

Map 6. Distribution of Subarctic Tribes in the Nineteenth Century
Athapaskan speakers were the principal inhabitants of the Northwestern and North-Central areas and of interior Alaska. Some Athapaskans, such as the Sarsi and Chilcotin, also extended southwards onto the plains of Alberta and into the Plateau region of British Columbia, which are outside the scope of this book.

Plate 18. Late-Prehistoric Bone and Antler Weapons, Northwestern Area
At lower right is a bunt, or stunning point, and in the top row centre are two barbed arrowheads with tapered conical stems. Most of the other specimens are prongs or tips for spears, the longest measuring 22 cm.

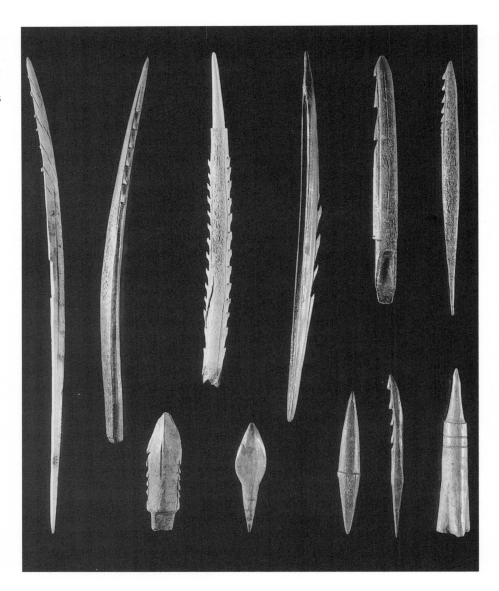

Plate 19. Heavy Stone Tools from the Yukon Large adzes, grooved for hafting, may have been used to split wood, as the chopping axe appears to have been unknown in the Subarctic. Of the three adzes shown here, the largest is 20.3 cm long. The grooved block at top left is a shaft-smoother, used to finish arrow and spear shafts.

Plate 20. Antler Spoon A unique artifact, this spoon was found at the Rat Indian Creek site in the northern Yukon; it is 18.7 cm long.

Creek or Rat Indian Creek sites in the northern Yukon. There, on the banks of the Porcupine River, they intercepted the migrating caribou that were returning northwards. This hunting pattern had been followed in these localities for centuries, possibly for millennia.

Together, the remains from these three sites document the last eleven centuries of prehistory and the first decades of European contact. Characteristic items include the following: large hide-scraping stones (chithos), numerous flakes bevelled at the edges for use as scrapers, endscrapers, and the occasional heavy ground-stone splitting adze, which served as a kind of axe. Double-bitted adzes were often pointed at the ends like picks, and are traditionally called war picks. They are a distinctive Athapaskan trait, found throughout nearly the entire Yukon River drainage. The antler tomahawk with knife-shaped chipped-stone blade, mentioned in legends, has not yet been found in archaeological sites, but some were collected for museums by European explorers. Small, stemmed arrow points are also distinctive tools of the late-prehistoric and early-historical Athapaskans in northern Alaska and the Yukon.

Though these northerners had a stone-age culture, some of them used stone only for heavy tools, such as splitting adzes and large hide-scrapers, while bone, antler and copper figured prominently in the fabrication of smaller items. They hammered native copper into arrowheads, other implements, and ornaments. Thanks to flooding at several riverbank sites in the northern Yukon, many finely made bone and antler objects were preserved under riverine mud. These include spoons or scoops, decorated beamers used for scraping hides, long slender points for arrows and spears, fishhooks, ornamental pendants, and a fish effigy or lure. The preservation of large amounts of bone refuse leads one to conclude that the main purpose of these camps was to hunt and process caribou for food, clothing, and shelter materials.

There is little recovered evidence of late-prehistoric dwellings. Nor should we expect to find permanent winter houses at the seasonally occupied riverside camps, though hearths consisting of accumulations of ash and charcoal are numerous. It is not known for certain that people cooked outdoors or, if not, what kind of shelter was associated with the hearths. Small-to-medium-size pits, now partly filled with refuse and buried beneath accumulated soil, may

Plate 21. Decorated Bone Objects from the Yukon The principal forms of artistic expression among early-historical northern Athapaskans are found in their clothing, songs and legends, but in the northwest their late-prehistoric antecedents often decorated bone implements. Shown at top and bottom left are fragments of fleshers, toothed at one end, the longest of which measures 18 cm. Between them are fragments of two beamers, which are a type of draw knife used in preparing skins; a complete beamer is illustrated in Plate 27. The smaller items are a bone tube or bead (top), two pendants perforated at one end, and (bottom) a knife handle for a sideways-hafted blade.

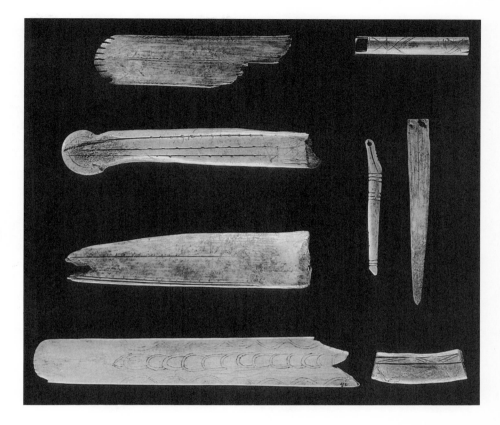

have been used to store food in the natural refrigerator of the semi-frozen ground. Smudges could have been kindled in smaller pits for smoking hides stretched on domed willow frames.

Northern Archaic occupation of the northern Yukon directly preceded the late-prehistoric period. As in the southern Yukon, there probably was cultural continuity, but Kutchin speakers may not have always lived in the northern Yukon. Whether the changes that occurred during the 2 000 years preceding European contact reflect ongoing development in the local population or whether other people began to hunt and settle in the area is a matter for discussion. Nevertheless, comparable changes were taking place over wide areas of the North. That is to say, there was an "updating" of tool styles and technology that transcended local and tribal boundaries and moderated differences between groups.

The Mackenzie Delta Region: Kutchin Antecedents

Traces of Kutchin camps at Whirl Lake, close to the Mackenzie Delta, and farther east on the plains between the Mackenzie and Anderson rivers antedate the arrival of Europeans, some of them by several centuries. The inhabitants of this region throughout historical times have been the Mackenzie Flats Kutchin, some of whom now live at Arctic Red River on the Mackenzie. At each locality there are housepits—the sunken floors of semisubterranean winter dwellings. On the Anderson Plain, birch-bark basket-trays holding finely fragmented bones from food animals were found in small pits. This mode of disposal evidently was a prescribed way of showing respect for the spirits of the animals that humans hunted to survive. Almost nothing was found on the nearby housepit floors.

The oblong sunken floor of the shelter at Whirl Lake was more productive. Together with the surrounding area and a cache pit, it yielded a crumpled birch-bark tray, shreds of stitched clothing of moose or caribou hide, and numerous implements. Near one end of the floor was a simple hearth. Though the shelter is less than 300 years old, no structural timbers remain. The archaeologist who excavated it suggests that a skin-covered dome had been erected over the pit. If so, the shelter would have been very different than the Anderson Plain houses, whose traces of heavy beams suggest that they probably supported a low roof covered with insulating turf and

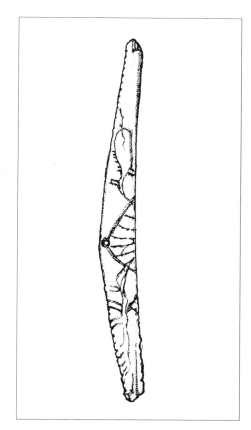

Plate 22. Decorated Bone Object
Possibly a snowshoe netting needle, it contains depictions of stylized animals and an unidentified feature. This 10-cm-long artifact is from the late-prehistoric Whirl Lake site at the head of the Mackenzie Delta.

dirt. The one-house camp at Whirl Lake yielded a heterogeneous collection of refuse, including bones of pike, waterfowl, moose, caribou, muskrat, beaver, and dog or wolf. The most outstanding item recovered is a needle, decorated with zoomorphic and other designs, for weaving the babiche (caribou-skin) netting of snowshoes (Plate 22). The crumpled birch-bark basket-tray has seamless folded corners like those on the Anderson Plain, but is much larger— equivalent to two sheets of letter-size stationery placed side by side. Basket-trays were made from single large sheets of bark folded at the corners. This seamless construction technique is common to the Yukon and Alaska, but was little used east of the Cordillera except in the Mackenzie Delta region.

At Whirl Lake the implements were very roughly prepared. They include crude scrapers, chopper tools, and fragments of knives. The camp may have been used during more than one season of the year. Bird bones and fly-larval casts among the fish bones in the cache pit suggest summer occupation, but the sunken house is a winter-type dwelling.

The Southwestern Yukon: Precursors of the Southern Tutchone

In the first millennium of our era, a powerful volcanic explosion thundered across the headwaters of the White River. Trillions of tonnes of volcanic ash were blasted out of Mount Bona at the southern end of the present Yukon-Alaska border. The ash plume blackened the sky, and blanketed the southern Yukon with a layer of grit that reached into the Northwest Territories. This ash layer, which fell in about A.D. 700—1 300 years ago—is called the White River Ash. Its thickness varies according to distance from the vent, but even today, after compaction, the pale-coloured ash is about 20 centimetres thick as far away as Carmacks. People had to flee the most heavily blanketed area, between the Alaska border and the present locations of Whitehorse and Carmacks. They had to move into territories occupied by others, whether friend or foe, as their own land had become uninhabitable and the game had been decimated or temporarily driven out.

Surprisingly, the stricken area was reoccupied within a few years. It is not known whether the pre-fall inhabitants returned or a new people arrived, but their technology was much the same. The reoccupation seems to have occurred as soon as conditions permitted. We know from latter-day eruptions, such as the Katmai in Alaska in 1912, that grasses and other vegetation emerge within a couple of years from even a very heavy ashfall. Temporarily though, moose, mountain sheep and caribou must have found the grit-covered chemically contaminated shrubs extremely unpalatable, and other animals and fish would have suffered distress in innumerable ways. However, no lasting effect on Subarctic prehistory has been discovered to substantiate speculation that the White River ashfall prompted widespread Athapaskan migrations. The ash layer does make a very good stratigraphic indicator that serves to designate the beginning of the late-prehistoric period.

Although the White River ashfall may not have triggered extensive migrations, tribal territories were not static in prehistoric times. The discontinuous distribution of Athapaskan speakers in historical times includes not only the subarctic Athapaskans but also several small tribes located in southern British Columbia and the Pacific Coast region of the United States, as well as populous interior tribes who live as far south as Mexico, the Navajo for instance. Their far-flung distribution is circumstantial evidence of past treks out of the North. But it is difficult if not impossible to trace these migrations through the archaeological evidence of simple stone tools alone. The most recent changes in territory and culture have been documented or retrieved from oral tradition, as when the Sarsi Athapaskans of Alberta adopted the Plains lifeways in historical times.

In the southern Yukon, a late-prehistoric people named Aishihik (after the lake west of Whitehorse) continued to use the implement forms of their antecedents—flaked knives and tabular hide-working stones (chithos) for example. However, during this time craftsmen started to make copper arrowheads, awls and other tools. Large dagger-like copper knives were especially prized, and are mentioned in legends; there are a few specimens in museums, collected in historical times. The Aishihik felled trees for shelters and fuel with large ground-stone adzes by striking vertical splinters of wood from around the trunk until the tree could be pushed over. Various projec-

Plate 23. Northwestern Stone Points
The stylistic range of stone tips from the Yukon and the Mackenzie River Valley is shown here. During the last thousand years, arrows, spears and lances have been tipped with heads or prongs of stone, copper, bone and antler. The point at lower right is 6.2 cm long.

Plate 24. Native Adaptations of European Materials and Goods

Europeans produced goods specifically for the fur trade, but Natives also adapted European materials to their own needs. The barbed iron harpoon-head from Teslin, Yukon (lower left), and the pair of stemmed brass points (far right) from Great Bear Lake are European trade goods. Many of the remaining items were produced locally by Native craftsmen, who recycled imported items for the metal they contained, as it was superior to bone and stone for particular tasks. The iron stunning points (third and fourth from top left) can be compared with the bone specimen in Plate 18. The cartridge case crimped over the shaft fragment (next to the brass points) is a style of blunt point developed, perhaps independently, at several locations across northern North America. Crooked knives (top, second from right) were manufactured both in European factories and locally by Natives from files and recycled metal. The large perforated oval is the top of a gunpowder can, removed and discarded. The small scraper above the oval and the scoop-shaped object below it are folded from sheet metal such as that obtained from powder cans. At top right is a small iron chisel. Aside from an end-hafted iron knife blade (second from top left), the other objects are iron projectile points or prongs. The harpoon head is 17.7 cm long.

tile points, often flaked from volcanic glass, included stemmed and side-notched points used to tip bone and antler arrowheads. Such points appeared in small sizes in many parts of the Subarctic during the last 800 years of prehistory, signalling a greater reliance on the bow and arrow. In historical times, the Aishihik adopted European technology and ways of doing things. Speakers of an Athapaskan language, they were named the Southern Tutchone by Europeans.

Other peoples now living in the region speak a different language, and thus must derive from a different origin. These Inland Tlingit live today in an area straddling the Yukon-British Columbia border. They may be a mixture of Tlingit who moved inland from the Alaska coast and an Athapaskan group that adopted many elements of Tlingit culture, including language. Their prehistory is, as yet, unknown. The influence of coastal peoples was especially great in the early historical period. During the 1800s, and perhaps earlier, Tlingit traders were taking both Native coastal products and European goods inland to exchange for furs. They reinforced trading connections by arranging marriages of family members to prominent inland customers. Coastal relations with the Athapaskan-speaking Tagish, who lived south of the present city of Whitehorse, were so close that the Tagish became bilingual, and by the present century Tlingit speech predominated. Many coastal customs, particularly those governing social relationships, also reached the interior in the same manner, probably along with some of the technology.

However, coastal trade did not lead to the formation of large, powerful inland tribes and villages; the land could not support them. Late-prehistoric campsites in the southern Yukon are smaller than those found in the northern Yukon along the Porcupine River or than those of the preceding Northern Archaic people. Inland hunting and camping groups must have been very small, rarely returning to the same sites. Early explorers often painted a dismal picture of Indian life in the southern Yukon. During the Little Ice Age of the eighteenth and nineteenth centuries, the climate became colder than it had been at any time during the previous 10 000 years. The late-prehistoric and historical Indians of the southern Yukon had to cope with the most demanding conditions that had prevailed in centuries.

Plate 25. Native Recycling in Nineteenth-Century America The pan at bottom was folded in the manner of a birch-bark basket from recycled sheet metal, and the large spear or lance head from Great Bear Lake was fashioned from a file. A broad knife (centre), comparable to the Eskimo ulu, was made from the wall of a copper pot still displaying the original handle-attaching lug. With its top removed, the gunpowder can served as a container. Length of the pan is 15.5 cm.

Subsistence Lifeways

Interpretations of the lives and lifeways of ancient times are less likely to stray from reality if they are confined to matters related to subsistence. This is especially true of the Subarctic, where very little of the archaeological data relates directly to the ritual, social and political life of past eras. Because of pronounced regional differences in resources, subsistence lifeways will be considered anew each time we move to another of our three Subarctic areas. The reconstruction offered here is based on native life at the time Europeans arrived in the Subarctic, discounting as much as possible the changes brought about by the fur trade. A safe assumption is that the reconstruction will be more reliable for the late millennia than for the earlier periods; it cannot be applied at all to the Ice Age occupation of Beringia.

Subsistence lifeways are closely tied to the environment— to the resources the land has to offer and to climate, vegetation and topography. It is the subsistence lifeway that most influences settlement pattern or campsite location, but the presence of hostile or friendly neighbours can also be important. Patterns and techniques of subsistence used in marginal areas tend to persist through time and to be shared between peoples if environmental conditions do not change. Sparse Subarctic resources could only support a low level of political or individual control over food harvesting and stored supplies. Nevertheless, according to traditional native accounts, industrious, intelligent men with leadership abilities frequently did attract a following and took over the direction of camp activities, such as the hunt and the installation and operation of fish weirs and caribou traps.

Survival in the Subarctic required a set seasonal round or cycle of subsistence activities and related travel. People had to be at the right place at the right time to find migrating game or intercept a run of fish. Accordingly, the following reconstruction of lifeways in the north-western Subarctic is chronological, beginning with the start of the year's activities in the spring.

Spring

As the days became longer and brighter in April, families and households that had camped together during the winter packed their gear on small hand-drawn sleds and toboggans and moved to spring

Plate 26. Scrapers and Knives from the Yukon These stone objects were prepared in the unifacial mode, and many are simply flakes shaped or retouched along the edges. A perforator or gouge is shown at lower right. The knife at top left is 13 cm long.

camps. There, they lived under skin tents and in huts constructed of saplings—usually two families at a camp. They concentrated on fishing and on trapping beaver and muskrat or shooting them with multipronged arrows. Beaver and muskrat not only were prized as food but yielded furs that could be traded to coastal peoples.

At first there was snow everywhere, but the landscape changed rapidly during the next few weeks with the increasing hours of sunshine. As the season progressed, people departed from spring camp by boat for other locations where fishing was better or to hunt. Fish traps and weir panels, cached the previous year, were repaired and placed in lake outlets. Gill nets, woven of bast, an inner-bark willow fibre, were also used. Several species of whitefish were taken in quantity from the streams, along with pike and other species. By this time, migratory waterfowl were arriving from the south. Geese, swans and other fowl fell prey to men armed with bows and arrows (unknown during earlier periods) or multipronged spears. As during other seasons, hunters also killed and ate any large game they could find.

Ice in the larger rivers usually went out between late April and late May. As there was little point in leaving spring camp immediately after breakup for a summer camp on the banks of a large, swollen river, most people stayed in the hinterlands, hunting, building canoes, scraping hides, and doing other tasks that they would be too busy to do during the brief summer. Old campsites are often found at plausible spring locations—the shores of small and medium-size lakes, and along inlet and outlet streams.

A major effort was made in parts of the country at this time to intercept the caribou migration northwards. Depending upon local circumstances, people congregated to hunt at caribou fences or at traditional river crossings, for instance near the Klo-kut and Rat Indian Creek sites on the Porcupine River.

Summer

In the northwestern Subarctic, nearly everyone went to fish camps on the main rivers or major tributaries. The exceptions were a few bands and families living in the hilly headwater regions or on the Arctic Slope in the Yukon and Alaska, who continued to hunt caribou and to fish in small streams.

Plate 27. Hide-working Tools Used in the Northwestern Area from Prehistoric Times to the Present

Northern peoples relied on well-tanned hides for clothing and other items essential to survival. Other than metal scraper-bits and Lysol soap as a tanning agent, there was little that European technology could provide to improve on Indian tanning methods. Shown here, at left, are three tabular stone scrapers, often called chithos, that imparted a suede-like finish. At bottom right is a bone flesher, 25 cm long, with one end bevelled to a bit. Above it is a beamer, or draw knife, and above that a long, thin blade that may have been either a skinning tool or a flesher. The smallest item is a bone awl.

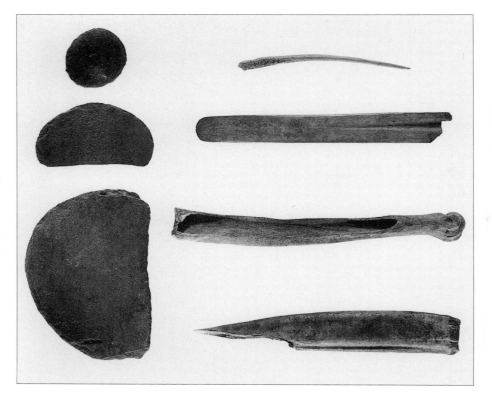

Normally, several families lived together in summer camps, fishing primarily for salmon except in the Mackenzie River drainage, though other fish were also caught. The installation and operation of traps and weirs was a group enterprise under the direction of a leader. Other fishing techniques were used locally, such as drifting with large dip nets in canoes, and dip-netting from platforms along the shore. When the salmon arrived, the women, and occasionally the men too, spent a large part of their time cutting and drying fish for coming months.

The low-lying banks of large rivers do not provide the best conditions for the survival of prehistoric remains. Some fishing camps were on gravel shores that were swept clean each year by floods; others have been eroded away or hidden by shifts in river courses. Sites do survive in some regions. The Moosehide, Fort Reliance and other sites along the Yukon River near Dawson appear to have been salmon-fishing camps in summer as well as rendezvous points at other times.

When possible, most able-bodied men left the big fishing camps for short periods to hunt. These forays probably explain the many small overnight sites that yield little more than a hearth, a lost or broken spear point or two, and a few stone chips from reshaping some tool.

In areas where there were few salmon, or if the salmon run failed, traps were installed on smaller rivers to take whitefish, suckers, grayling, some pike, or other species. A number of sites plausibly situated for these activities have been found, but such alternative summer sites were sometimes at the same location as fall camps. Late in the summer people went berrying, sometimes picking enough blueberries and low-bush cranberries to keep in large birch-bark baskets stored in pits in the ground.

Autumn and Early Winter

Around mid-September, families moved to autumn camps. These were usually situated away from the main rivers, as at a lake outlet, where one is almost assured of finding an ancient campsite. Again, traps were placed in the stream for small whitefish and grayling. While the women and children tended the fish traps and snared small game near the camp, the men went out on short hunting trips.

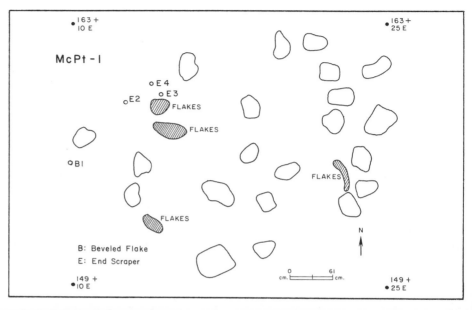

McPt - I

- •163 +
  10 E
- •163 +
  25 E

- ○E 4
- ○E 3
- ○E2

FLAKES

FLAKES

○B1

FLAKES

FLAKES

N

B: Beveled Flake
E: End Scraper

0   61
cm. |———|———| cm.

- •149 +
  10 E
- •149 +
  25 E

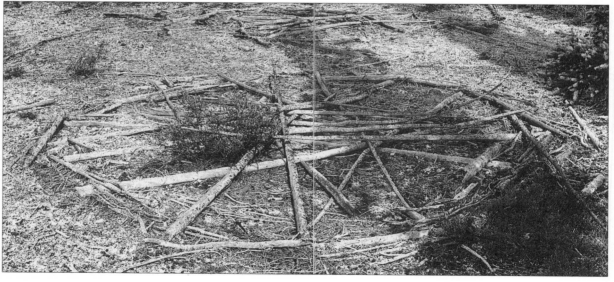

Plate 28. The Conical Shelter through the Ages *Top Left*: Drawing of boulders once used as tent weights, Great Bear Lake. This buried feature, which was discovered and excavated by the author, may be several thousand years old. *Bottom left*: Pole supports remaining from a collapsed conical shelter, Great Bear Lake, probably late nineteenth century (Photograph by the author). *Above*: A conical shelter near Rae on Great Slave Lake, 1913 (Photograph by J.A. Mason, CMC neg. 26058).

The gathering of tool-making materials was an important activity. Because of the high upland location of sources and the wide dispersal of material over the surface, it was necessary to gather native copper, obsidian (volcanic glass), chert and other preferred types of stone when the ground was free of snow. Some people made excursions to acquire these materials, but the food quest was paramount, and stops at such locations would have been worked in with other travel. Nevertheless, major campsite clusters and flaking stations are found at such raw-material sources. Examples are the obsidian-flaking stations at Batza Téna in Alaska, and Mount Edziza in British Columbia; the silicified-shale source at the junction of the Thunder River and the lower Mackenzie River north of present Fort Good Hope; the fused-tuff outcrops southwest of Fort Norman in the western Mackenzie District; and farther east, on the edge of the Barren Grounds, the Acasta site, where people went to make quartzite tools.

The sharp night frosts of October drove all the people not out on the fall caribou hunt into their winter shelters, which were often at the autumn camp. These were turf-covered and half-underground structures in Alaska, parts of the Yukon, and the northwestern Mackenzie District. Because of the distinctive dwelling type, the autumn/winter sites are among the easiest to identify as to season of occupation. Such dwellings have been excavated near Dawson, where they date to historical times, at the Old Chief Creek and Rat Indian Creek sites in the northern Yukon, at Whirl Lake and on the Anderson Plain in the northwestern Mackenzie District, and in Alaska. Closed-in double lean-tos built of small trees were common in the Yukon and the western Mackenzie District. Solid-walled, conical wooden lodges were built in some localities in the same region, from either closely spaced vertical poles or spruce saplings. The domed portable lodge, used historically in the central and northern parts of both the Yukon and Alaska, may have been a house for all seasons, as any number of caribou hides could be added to shed rain and provide the insulation needed for a warm interior. Hide-covered frames may have been the only practical housing during early times or where little wood was available. Winter communities were small, often consisting of only one or two households, though neighbours might be only a few kilometres distant. When dwellings decayed or were moved, the only

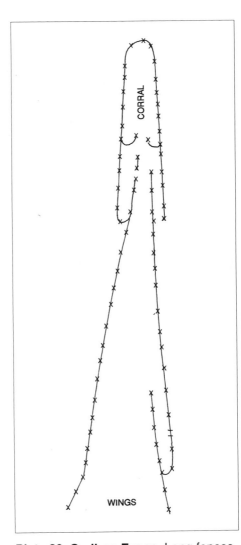

CORRAL

WINGS

Plate 29. Caribou Fence Long fences guided caribou into corrals, where they were snared and lanced. This diagram traces the outline of a classic Kutchin caribou fence and corral of the northern Yukon Territory. The fence is 3.2 km long, but only the wings adjoining the corral are shown here.

evidence the archaeologist finds of their existence is the few articles left behind on the floors.

Caribou of the Porcupine herd arrived from the north late in the fall, usually shortly before freeze-up. Local bands intercepted the migration as the quickly moving animals passed through. Elsewhere there were smaller herds, as in the Fortymile River area near Dawson. Several men, together with their families, went to the hills for the caribou. There they refurbished the caribou fences, some of which were in long, straight lines with openings into which noose snares were set. Better known are the caribou corrals with long wings that led into well-constructed surrounds. Men lanced animals caught in nooses set in the corral and shot others that were milling around inside the surround. Such devices were used throughout the Subarctic, and were adapted to take moose and mountain sheep. The continent-wide distribution of fences and drives suggests that their use is very ancient. In addition to communal efforts, there was also a lot of ambushing, stalking and running down of game by individuals. Traces of caribou fences built in historical times have been studied in the northern Yukon and adjacent Alaska and in the northern Mackenzie District. Earlier fences have disappeared through decay, but there must have been camps located near fences, just as there were in historical times. In one instance, at Great Bear Lake, ravines that channelled the caribou are incorporated into the caribou fence and trap. The presence of numerous prehistoric campsites near the fences there suggests that caribou fences built in more ancient times had also incorporated the area's ravines.

Winter to Early Spring

During October and November the rivers and lakes froze over. Throughout the rest of the darkening days of early winter, hunting continued but with less concerted effort than before. Women and children set snares for hare and ptarmigan. They also fished through the ice with spears, lures and hooks, and with nets set under the ice. Fishing continued until the ice grew unmanageably thick or most fish had left for the deeper waters of larger rivers and lakes. When the shortest winter days arrived there was little hunting, trapping or fishing. Cold as it was, people often travelled at this time of year to visit nearby relatives and friends.

Late in January or during February, when little of the stored food remained, most members of the family left on an extended hunting-foraging trip, but the old people who stayed behind had to get along as best they could. This was an especially hungry time of the year, and it was not unusual for several families to travel and camp together. In the daytime the men went their separate ways, hunting hare, porcupine, spruce grouse and, if they could find any, caribou, moose and (in early times) bison. The people kept moving, but if they got a moose or bison they stayed near the kill site for several days. About the first of April, they went back to their winter quarters. They did not stay long, and later in the month left for spring camps or to hunt caribou.

Though prehistoric life was punctuated by the events occurring at specific places, its essential dimensions were time (season) and type of activity—"They were going down to the mouth of the stream after breakup." As for place, the whole land was the site, used repeatedly according to a traditional pattern.

Having introduced readers to Canada's first inhabitants, our narrative has reached the threshold of history in the Northwestern Area. Before moving back in time again to examine the course of prehistory in other parts of the Canadian Subarctic, we will examine a subject in which Native peoples in general had a strong interest—trade in goods and materials. In the next chapter the focus is on the Northwestern Area, where trade is best documented through traditional and historical accounts, but it was an important activity right across the Canadian Subarctic, even in early prehistoric times.

4. Prehistoric Trade

A lot of trading went on throughout the Subarctic despite the self-sufficiency of Native societies. Evidence of prehistoric trade is provided by archaeologists in the form of foreign or exotic materials and goods found at ancient campsites, and by the early historical accounts of Europeans. These accounts indicate that, at first, the Europeans were cheerfully integrated into existing Native trade networks because they brought new goods that could be fed into the system by Native middlemen. However, as white traders moved deeper into the hinterlands, they aroused the hostility of Natives whose power they were threatening and whose trade they were disrupting. This resentment was vigorously expressed. In 1852, for example, Tlingit traders from the coast of Alaska travelled 400 kilometres to destroy a competing Hudson's Bay Company post at Fort Selkirk in the Yukon.

The extent to which trade links were developed and defended in historical times suggests that barter had very deep roots in Native societies. That food and other Native products were also important in aboriginal trade dispels any notion that trade was a recent activity or was only based on exchanging furs for imported European goods.

Nevertheless, life in the North could have been sustained without commerce. Although instances have been recorded of starving bands bartering for food from better-supplied groups, that kind of dependence does not characterize the economy of the Subarctic. There were varied incentives for trade other than the exchange of goods. For one thing, trade helped to satisfy the consuming interest in travel among many northern peoples, especially the western Athapaskans, who often travelled for weeks to see new places and things. Moreover, the mechanisms of trade, such as partnerships and intertribal gatherings, provided a means of travelling safely into the territory of another, potentially hostile, group. Trade also made it possible to obtain scarce items that served as status symbols, for instance dentalia, or tooth shells, from Vancouver Island. Other prestige items included some of the foods that would be served at social or ceremonial gatherings, such as memorial feasts for the dead.

Services, such as those of a shaman, or medicine man, were also exchanged locally for goods or other services. It is not always possible to distinguish between local trade within a band and long-distance trade, the type usually recognized in the archaeological

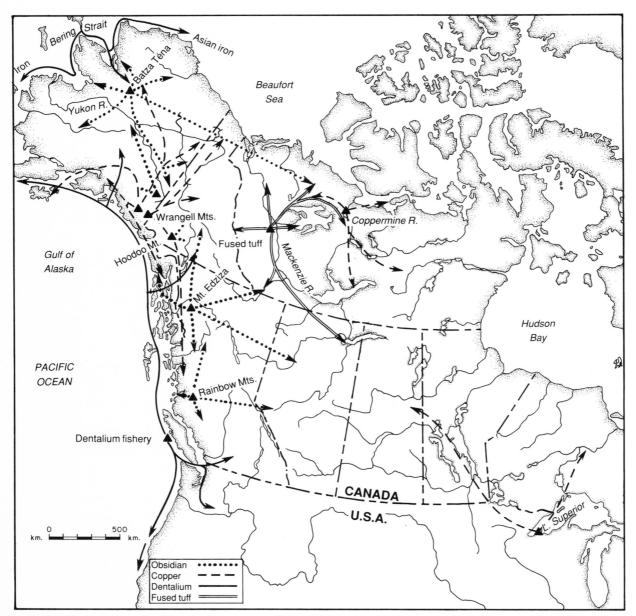

Bering Strait

Iron

Asian iron

Batza Téna

Yukon R.

Beaufort Sea

Wrangell Mts.

Fused tuff

Coppermine R.

Gulf of Alaska

Hoodoo Mt.

Mackenzie R.

Mt. Edziza

Hudson Bay

PACIFIC OCEAN

Rainbow Mts.

Dentalium fishery

CANADA

U.S.A.

L. Superior

0   500
km.   km.

Obsidian · · · · · ·
Copper – – – – –
Dentalium ————
Fused tuff ═══════

Map 7. Prehistoric Trade The arrows indicate the movement of selected trade goods between their source locations and the campsites where they were found. Their appearance at distant sites in the form of either the raw material or finished goods is a reliable indicator of the extent of such trade between Native peoples.

80

record. A limited distribution of a material, such as obsidian (used to make arrow points and knives), may simply reflect the territorial range of a single band controlling the source of the material. A wider distribution, however, provides plausible evidence for long-distance trade in this material.

Perhaps of greater interest are the mechanisms through which trade was conducted. Historical accounts can give us some idea of what might have gone on during prehistoric times. But before we discuss these processes, it may be helpful to examine some of the items exchanged in Native trade.

The Goods Traded

Perishables

Most prehistoric trade was probably in foodstuffs or in materials that did not survive long. In British Columbia, eulachon fish oil was so important in the trade between coastal tribes and those of the Subarctic interior that the routes from the coast are popularly called "grease trails." Major grease trails led up the Alsek, Chilkat, Taku and Nass rivers into northern British Columbia and the Yukon. Were it not for information compiled by explorers and ethnographers, we would not have known of this activity nor of the Tagish-Tlingit trade, which is discussed more fully later in this chapter. Nor would the archaeological record have revealed that a Yukon-valley tribe traded straight-grained spruce to a Yukon-plateau tribe for use in arrows. Upland spruce tends to grow with a twist, though it is hard to believe that there was *no* straight-grained spruce in the Yukon uplands. Instead, there may have been a rudimentary focus on regional efficiency that, in turn, helped maintain trade as a social activity. In another case, one in which the archaeological record was preserved, birch bark was found at the prehistoric-Inuit site of Nadluk, evidently having been obtained in trade from the forest that begins more than 200 kilometres to the south.

Obsidian

Volcanic glass is not as hard as flint but is much easier to flake, and it forms extremely sharp edges. It served well for points, knives and skin-scrapers, though tougher and harder stone is better for such work as adzing and drilling. Natural occurrences of obsidian are scattered along the Coast Mountains and elsewhere in the Cordilleran region, where there has been volcanic activity during the last several million years. Chemically, each flow differs slightly from all others, especially in the proportion of trace elements. Thus, the source of obsidian artifacts can be precisely identified through analysis of trace elements and comparison with geological outcrops.

Subarctic peoples used obsidian derived from approximately ten sources located in Alaska, the southwestern Yukon and British Columbia. Some outcrops were more intensively exploited than others, and obsidian from them was more widely traded. The most important sources were those in the Koyukuk River drainage of northwestern Alaska and the several obsidian flows at Mount Edziza, or "Ice Mountain," which is near the Stikine River in northern British Columbia, not far from the coast. Lesser sources are located north of the Wrangell Mountains in eastern Alaska and in the low mountains at the eastern end of Kluane National Park in the Yukon. A small amount of obsidian from Rainbow Peak near Anahim Lake in west-central British Columbia reached the southern edge of the Subarctic, overlapping that from Mount Edziza to the north. However, not all tested archaeological specimens have been traced to known outcrops of raw material; evidently some sources have yet to be identified.

Blocks and nodules of obsidian can be picked up from the surface of an outcrop and in adjacent stream beds, so it was not necessary for prehistoric peoples to actually quarry or mine the volcanic glass. These chunks were sometimes carried away to be traded or processed elsewhere. Usually, though, implements were roughed out at the source to reduce the amount of material that had to be transported and later discarded as chipping waste. This activity left thick scatters of waste flakes and shattered nodules near the source, but few identifiable implements. Sometimes it was necessary to go on a long trek to high, remote country to obtain the raw material. Obsidian sources may have been controlled by individual bands, as was copper in the far west. If so, to avoid trouble it would have been necessary to get permission from the band that controlled access to the source. However, the Subarctic was sparsely settled, and it may have been possible to poach a raw material without being detected.

Koyukuk River obsidian from the Batza Téna source was traded throughout Alaska north of the Alaska Range as early as 10 700 years ago, and small quantities of it also reached the Yukon. Tiny chips of Batza Téna obsidian recovered in the Mackenzie District northwest of Great Bear Lake probably came from the sharpening of a tool that had passed eastwards through many hands. The outcrops are located in Athapaskan Indian territory, but Batza Téna obsidian was traded to Palaeo-Eskimos from 4 000 to 2 000 years ago and occasionally to later Eskimos in western Alaska. Mount Edziza obsidian was also traded very widely. Trade networks that ran both along the Pacific coast and inland through the Rocky Mountains brought material from this upland volcano to a number of unrelated tribes. Edziza obsidian was being used along Glacier Bay on the Alaska coast northwest of Juneau nearly 10 000 years ago, in east-central British Columbia and the southern Yukon by 6 000 years ago, and in the southwestern Mackenzie District perhaps not long thereafter.

Fused Tuff

A unique glassy material, fused tuff was obtained from the hills near Stewart and Tate lakes, southwest of present Fort Norman in the Mackenzie River valley. This variety flaked somewhat like obsidian. It is a pretty rock that occurs in lustrous grey shades, and cream and taupe hues suggestive of vanilla and caramel puddings. Flakes and tools made of fused tuff have been found in a few northern Alberta sites and all through the western Mackenzie District except along the Arctic coast. Small amounts, perhaps already made into tools, also reached the central Mackenzie District and the Yukon. A cache of large fused-tuff flakes, perhaps someone's trading stock, was found at the outlet of Great Bear Lake. Some of these finds are at least 6 000 years old. Native exploitation of the source was still faintly remembered by Dene (Athapaskans) living in the region, nearly 150 years after they had ceased using the material for their knives and arrowheads.

Native Copper

Natural metallic copper in the Subarctic comes from two principal areas. One is the Wrangell Mountains region of Alaska, adjacent to the southwest corner of the Yukon. Yukon tribes recovered copper nuggets from the gravels of a headwaters tributary of the White River near the Alaska-Yukon border; on the other side of the mountains, Alaskan bands exploited sources in the Copper River drainage. Access to the copper was controlled by local Southern Tutchone and Ahtna Indians. The Southern Tutchone traded copper to their neighbours in the interior, among them the Tagish, who then traded the copper to the coastal Tlingit, who in turn moved it southwards to other coastal groups. The Tlingit also got copper through trade links with the Ahtna.

Another major source of copper is a broad zone of the northern Mackenzie District close to the Arctic coast. It extends from the Dismal Lakes eastwards to Bathurst Inlet. Other sources—those on Victoria Island and at Lake Superior—are outside the scope of this book. Both Copper Inuit and Yellowknife Athapaskans collected copper at scattered localities where it had weathered out of rock outcrops. Copper-working technology and trade in native copper began at about the same period in both the Yukon-Alaska-British Columbia area and the Northwest Territories. Archaeological evidence for this trade does not date back very far in the far west, probably to no earlier than 800 years ago. However, a few older specimens, from the first millennium A.D., have been reported from the central Mackenzie District.

Dentalium

Prized dentalia shells, shaped like miniature elephant tusks, come from the coast of Vancouver Island, and were more widely traded in North America than any other product derived from a single area. Locally, they were used as currency. There is evidence that dentalia were being transported far into the Cordilleran region in prehistoric times, and beyond to the Aleutian Islands of Alaska. But confirmation of trade in the Western Subarctic came later through activities of the Hudson's Bay Company, the Russian-American Company, and Native traders who exchanged these shells. A variant form of a story about obtaining dentalia by sinking the corpse of a slave as bait into a deep Pacific Coast lake exists in northwestern Alaska, though it is hard to tell if this legend dates back to prehistoric times or was spread by later traders. Accounts recorded by Pacific Coast explorers state that dentalia were harvested off Vancouver Island by

Plate 30. Prehistoric Trade Goods

The fish effigy or lure is from the Kutchin campsite at Klo-kut in the northern Yukon. This bone carving may have been traded by, or received as a gift from, the Kobuk River Eskimos of northwestern Alaska, where nearly identical specimens were made. It is 16 cm long. At bottom is a small, oval-shaped birch-bark container, with inserted wooden bottom and a decorative design at the joined ends of the bark sheet. It was recovered from a late-nineteenth-century semisubterranean dwelling at Fort Reliance near Dawson, in Han Athapaskan territory. Similar objects have been collected in historical times from Eskimos in the vicinity of Bering Strait, who may have obtained them through trade with interior Indians. Other items include a Native-copper point; fused-tuff rocks (upper left and right) and spearhead (lower left); and a chunk of obsidian below and to the right of an obsidian point. Map 7 shows the sources and distribution of these materials.

sinking a dog carcass to the bottom as bait, whereas these shells were actually harvested with a type of rake or broom, or simply gathered from the shore after a storm.

Manufactures

At the time of European contact, Natives were trading baskets, ladles, wooden tubs, clothing, snowshoes and other manufactured items among themselves. Except in the permafrost of the High Arctic, this kind of material does not survive long in the ground unless it is rapidly buried under mud or flood silts. Therefore, we know little about prehistoric trade in local craft specialties. In addition to the exchange of items especially produced for trading, there may have been some gift-giving between individuals and bands. Expectations of reciprocity often place gift-giving in the category of trade. One striking case can be cited. A fish effigy from the late-prehistoric Klo-kut site in the northern Yukon is so similar to one from a site on the Kobuk River of northwestern Alaska that both can be attributed to a single source, and to possibly the same artisan. The two bone carvings are representations of grayling, carved in a highly distinctive manner that delineates scales, ribs and other details. One effigy is from an Athapaskan camp, the other from an Eskimo site located several hundred kilometres to the west, where both specimens may have originated, as other somewhat similar carvings have been found at Eskimo sites. Was this exceptional piece a gift to affirm a trading partnership?

From earliest prehistoric times onwards, Indians and Eskimos used red "paint" in several ways of ritual significance, for instance on clothing seams and for rock paintings. The pigment stone that was pulverized to powder to produce this stain was a hematite-rich rock that had to be baked before it could be crushed. Very few iron-rich rocks were satisfactory, and most were obtained through either local or long-distance trade.

The Mechanisms of Trade: A Sometimes Rough Diplomacy

What was the cultural and social significance of trade to the prehistoric societies of the Subarctic? Local specialities can create trading opportunities even in a homogenous area, but the greatest stimulus to trade occurs between dissimilar environmental zones offering different raw materials and manufactures. For example, obvious opportunities exist between the coast and adjacent interior. In the Yukon and northern British Columbia, interior peoples had contacts with the Pacific coast; in the northern Yukon and Northwest Territories, trade was with the Inuit and their Eskimo ancestors. Farther west—in Alaska—the Pacific, Arctic and interior peoples converged upon the most important trade zone of the North, the Bering Strait region between Asia and North America. Nearly 2 000 years ago, a little smelted iron and probably many other Asian goods reached the northwestern Subarctic via this route. By the early nineteenth century, with European items added to the mix of trade goods and with an indirect link to Eurasian fur markets, Eskimo and Chukchi trade fairs were being held near the Bering Strait. There were trade fairs elsewhere, for example at the mouth of the Nass River on the Pacific coast, where coastal and interior routes met. Nothing on that scale existed in the Subarctic, but intertribal gatherings did take place. Each year, people from several Athapaskan groups in Alaska and the Yukon gathered for trade and festivities at the confluence of the Yukon and Tanana rivers in Alaska.

We do not know if there were large multitribal meetings in the Canadian Subarctic. But certainly, Athapaskans met at different times with Crees, West Coast Indians, and Eskimos. In historical times, Cree and Athapaskan traders arrived at a rendezvous point or at the host camp with several well-armed retainers. If the hosts were weak or unwary, they often received little for their furs or had their camp pillaged. "Indeed, trading and raiding were closely connected in Kutchin [northern Athapaskan] thought; one kind of activity might easily be replaced by the other" (*Handbook of North American Indians*, Vol. 6: 522–23).

In Alaska, trading visits reportedly were more amicable. There and in the Yukon, transactions took place between trading partners. Athapaskans prearranged meetings in their territory with the coastal Tlingit, at Tagish and Kusawa lakes in the southwestern Yukon and at Dease Lake in northern British Columbia. The forests were immense, and the people had no way to reckon time precisely, so when the outsiders arrived at the meeting place they sent up smoke signals to

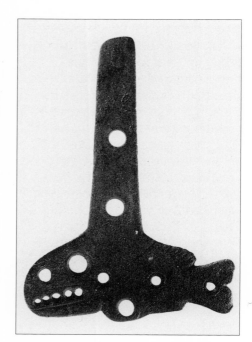

Plate 31. Stylized Killer Whale Made from imported iron, this 6-cm-high ornament was found on the Stikine River in British Columbia. Its discovery inland points to contact with coastal traders, especially the Tlingit, to whom the killer whale was an important symbol.

notify the people who lived or hunted in the area that they had arrived. Trading activities were accompanied by feasting, ceremonies, sports contests, and in some instances gambling. Relations between trading partners were usually amicable, involving courtesy exchanges of kinship titles, but this was not always the case. Often one or both trading partners behaved arrogantly, and tried to intimidate and cheat the other. In historical times, the overbearing group was usually the one with ties to the European traders, giving them access to the much-coveted foreign goods, which could be bartered at great profit. This led to resentment, sometimes culminating in murderous reprisals. Naturally, there were trade monopolies. The group that controlled one end of a route often controlled the trade. For example, few Athapaskan traders visited Tlingit territory on the Pacific coast, since the powerful Tlingit had assumed the role of middlemen and mounted their own expeditions to the interior.

One peculiar trading mechanism in parts of the North was *silent trade*, in which the principals did not come into direct personal contact. One party left trade goods at a predetermined spot and then withdrew a considerable distance away. The other arrived, selected the desired items, and left goods in exchange, which the first party collected some time later. Said by ethnologists to be a trade mechanism developed by hostile or fearful people, this superficially simple interaction must have required prior knowledge of the wants of the other party. It seems remarkable that purportedly antagonistic people who dared not meet would bother setting up commercial relations involving nonessential items, and that a trader would trudge a hundred kilometres or more through forest and rough terrain to find the exact spot where a bundle of goods had been left "on approval." Silent trade undoubtedly was an established procedure in antiquity, being well-suited to sparsely occupied land where people could not commit themselves a year in advance to meet at an appointed time and place.

Information on Native trade practices in the Subarctic is available for the Yukon, northern British Columbia, and Alaska. Similar arrangements may have existed east of the Rocky Mountains, but information is lacking. The reason may lie in the earlier establishment of European trading posts deep in the Subarctic interior, which destroyed any existing Native trade patterns before they could be recorded. However, a few clues remain to indicate that such patterns had indeed existed. For instance, the Chipewyan Athapaskans and many Cree became middlemen so readily in the trade with Europeans that there must have been an existing Native trade network. The Chipewyan acquired an astonishing number of knives from the Hudson's Bay Company post at Churchill, evidently to pass on to tribes like the Yellowknife and Dogrib, deep in the interior.

In the far west, however, intertribal trade persisted, perhaps because Native peoples maintained an interest in acquiring Native-produced goods, even such nonmaterial items as songs. Traditionally, the Tlingit of the coast and the Tagish of the Yukon interior exchanged dried clams, wooden boxes, dried seaweed, eulachon oil, ground-squirrel robes, lichen dyes and goat wool for blankets, tanned moose and caribou hides, native copper, and other finished items such as Athapaskan tanned clothing. Later European imports displaced only a few of these products.

5. The North-Central Area from Early to Middle Times
(8 000 to 3 500 Years Ago)

Our North-Central Area comprises the territory lying between Great Bear Lake, Great Slave Lake and Lake Athabasca on the west and Hudson Bay on the east. It incorporates the northern limits of the boreal forest, which cuts obliquely across the Northwest Territories, together with some of the adjacent Barren Grounds. During the past hundred years, Inuit have lived on the Barrens; Athapaskan Indians of the Chipewyan and Yellowknife tribes, though hunting there seasonally, spent most of the year in the forest. In earlier times, however, Athapaskan Indians were the main inhabitants of the southern parts of the Barrens. Their life was based on seasonal moves between Barrens and forest in pursuit of caribou, their main resource for food and hides. This lifeway may go back 8 000 years to the initial settlement of the region.

From the air, the land looks flat in the north—a mosaic formed by innumerable irregularly shaped patches and streaks of water, some tiny and some immense, set in a barren expanse—but in the south the terrain is supplied with texture by the dark boreal forest. The view from the ground is different though, the dominant feature being the hard bedrock of the Precambrian Shield. Scraped clean by Ice Age glaciers, Shield rock remains exposed in many places, forming a maze of features carved in a past age. Elsewhere, the layer of stony debris left long ago by melting ice sheets is here and there shaped into low hills and serpentine eskers, or reworked by rivers and wind into sandy patches. In some places the land is shrubby, in others forested, and elsewhere bare of all but the sparsest vegetation. Bogs fill low areas, and muskeg forms on surfaces where permafrost impedes drainage. Hills and bluffs, barely discernible from the air, rise to prominence, and wild rivers rush out of highlands, often confined between the rocky walls they have cut into the Shield rock.

Ten thousand years ago, the southern edge of the continental ice sheet lay east of Great Bear Lake and across the present Great Slave and Athabasca lakes, where it blocked glacial Lake McConnell from draining. From there the ice front curved southeastwards, damming another immense glacial lake, Agassiz. The melt continued, and within another 2 000 years, all the country west of Hudson Bay was open to settlement, though the shoreline was submerged below sea level.

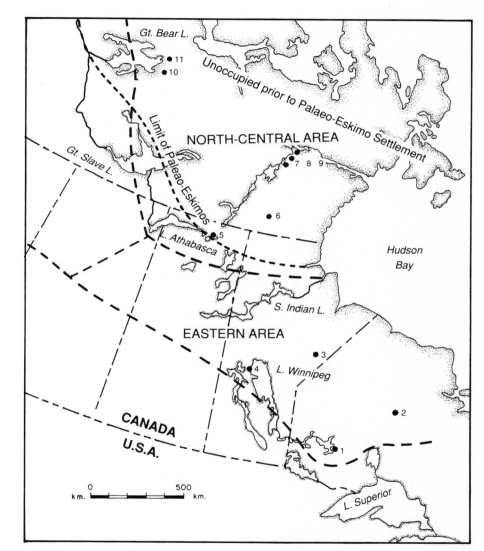

1 Eaka & Pelican Falls (Shield)
2 Quimet (Shield)
3 Gods Lake & Elk Island (Shield)
4 Grand Rapids (Shield)
5 Black Lake (trace N. Plano)
6 Blackfly Cove & Dot Island (N. Plano)
7 Grant Lake (N. Plano)
8 Migod (Shield, trace N. Plano)
9 Aberdeen (N. Plano, Shield)
10 Acasta Lake (Acasta phase)
11 Kamut Lake (mixed)

Map 8. Archaeological Sites in the North-Central and Eastern Areas The sites shown are from the early period and the later Shield culture. The southern limit of Palaeo-Eskimo penetration, following Shield withdrawal from the Keewatin, is also indicated.

As the glaciers melted and vegetation crept northwards, did herds of bison, caribou and other animals follow, pursued by early hunters? Some prehistorians suggest that events may not have been this simple. Deglaciation may have become so rapid that it threw the ecology into chaos, disrupting earlier hunting patterns adapted to plains and tundra. Initially, people may have been unable to make a living in the boreal forest. Thus, colonization of the North may have been more complex than assumed by some prehistorians.

Arrival of the Plano People

From the Rocky Mountains to the Atlantic coast, Late Palaeo-Indians, or Plano peoples, succeeded Clovis people after the end of the Ice Age, about 10 000 years ago (see Chapter 1). The Plano people of the Plains were best situated to colonize the Subarctic in the North-Central Area. Unfortunately, too few traces of their existence have been found in the boreal forest to convincingly document the northward Plano migration. Undated Plano spear points, of which there are many varieties, have been found in southern parts of the boreal forest, but constitute only a faint trail to mark the probable northward spread of Plano people. Perhaps hunting bands were so dispersed and constantly on the move in early times that little more than a few scattered discards ever will be found.

The type of Plano point best documented in the North is called the Agate Basin point. Such points found on the Plains usually date from between 9 500 and 8 500 years ago, but those in the North are barely 8 000 years old. The difference in age may represent the slow movement of Plano people into and through the forest to its northern edge. They had taken about the same amount of time to penetrate the boreal forest farther south in southeastern Manitoba and along the north shore of Lake Superior. Those who did penetrate the Subarctic to reach the edge of the Barren Lands are known as the Agate Basin Northern Plano.

The Agate Basin Northern Plano

This phase is known from sites located in the Barrens of the Keewatin District, extending into the Dubawnt and Thelon river drainage and a little way into the eastern Mackenzie District. The spruce forest then grew farther north, closer to the ancient camps on the Barrens, than it

Plate 32. Northern Plano Implements from the Keewatin District These specimens from the Grant Lake site include four Agate Basin-type lanceolate points (top row), a ground adze-bit (middle row left), two finely prepared endscrapers (lower centre), two asymmetrical biconvex edge-knives (lower right), a small stone wedge (centre), and a tabular circular tool (lower left). The latter type was probably used for scraping hides, judging by its similarity to later Athapaskan scrapers. The point at top right is 6.8 cm long.

does today. Camps were well situated for fishing and for hunting migrating caribou during the ice-free season. During the winter the inhabitants may have moved southwards into the forest, for instance into northern Saskatchewan. The forest would have provided shelter against the wind—bitterly cold even though the climate was warmer than it is today. Fuel for warmth and wood for building shelters and making implements also came from the forest. Radiocarbon dates for this occupation are not entirely consistent, but we are reasonably certain that, by 7 000 years ago, northern Plano people had been in the Keewatin for several centuries.

Artifacts and camp traces of these early people have been recovered. Implements include Agate Basin-style lanceolate spear points; large, broad, leaf-shaped biface knife blades; endscrapers, which are common to nearly every northern culture; and point fragments modified to form carving tools. The flat discs trimmed from thin sheets of quartzite may have been used to scrape hides in a manner similar to the way that historical and prehistoric Athapaskans used their large tabular stone scrapers (chithos). Many small pillow-shaped stones, so-called wedges, are also found; it is thought that they were hammered into bones to split them lengthways into long pieces for making implements. Another suggested use for wedges is as grooving-tool bits. Woodworking appears to have been important. Sandstone abraders were used to shape or finish antler or wood implements, and humped-back adzes with a ground bit are numerous, though represented mainly by fragments.

Camp remains abound in the Keewatin at Grant Lake, where there was a convergence of the esker ridges that migrating caribou followed. Agate Basin Plano people lived and hunted here during the summer. Stone implements and flake clusters are found in conjunction with hearths or fire-cracked rocks. These are the disturbed surviving record of living-floors once enclosed within hide-covered shelters. Boulder tent-weights, now scattered, surround the shelter traces. The shelters, no longer sharply defined, were four to five metres across and were probably oval or circular in outline.

Acasta Lake, Where West Meets East
As yet, the Acasta Lake complex has been identified only in the area between Great Bear Lake and the Coppermine River. Some prehis-

Plate 33. Implements of the Acasta Phase Shown here are two heavy Acasta scraping and chopping tools (bottom right; top second from left) and two large lance or knife blades (upper right). Their rough appearance is not the result of bad workmanship but of the material they are made from—a variety of quartzite that does not flake smoothly. From left to right in the middle row are a lobate-stemmed Kamut point, a slightly notched Acasta point, a lanceolate point roughly comparable to Agate Basin points, and a notched transverse burin. Such burins, including the two others at bottom row left, are a distinctive implement of both the Palaeo-Arctic (Microblade) culture of the northwest and the Acasta culture of the North-Central Area; they may have been used as scrapers or as bits to shape hard materials such as antler. At top left is a slug-shaped uniface, 8 cm long, attributed to the Acasta complex.

torians classify the 7 000-year-old complex as a variety of Northern Plano culture, but its origins may be more westerly than southern and Plano. Characteristic western styles of tools, that is Northern Cordilleran, are present. The transverse burins of the Acasta can be traced across the Yukon and into Alaska, and their lobate-stemmed spear points have early counterparts in the northern Yukon. Thus, the Acasta may represent an easterly branch of Northern Cordilleran people. Other distinctive artifacts include lanceolate spear points, very large stemmed endscrapers, large pointed lances or knives, single-edged semilunar-shaped knives, the rare drill or gouge, and heavy so-called scraper-planes or flaked adzes. Numerous simple hearths were found at Acasta Lake. One reason why people camped there, at the major Acasta site, was to make tools from chunks of quartzite detached from a huge boulder on a nearby ridge of glacial gravel. The rough or preliminary shaping of tools produced a lot of waste, making it expedient to work close to the source of the material. Charred bones of caribou, black bear, beaver, hare, eagle and two species of fish were recovered from a single large hearth, apparently used for roasting game in the ground. These reflect a broadly based hunting economy appropriate to the location of Acasta sites near the juncture of the boreal forest and the Barrens.

The Shield Culture

By 6 000 years ago, subtle changes in style and craftsmanship were creeping into the Agate Basin-style spear points used by Northern Plano people. There were other changes in their stone-tool technology, one of the most significant being the chipping of hafting notches into spear points. Before long the Northern Plano phased into the Shield culture (termed by archaeologists the Shield Archaic) west of Hudson Bay. The Caribou Lake Plano culture of southeastern Manitoba, known from finds made between Caribou Lake and the Winnipeg River, may represent a similar transition from Plano to Shield culture at the southern edge of the boreal forest. Characteristic Caribou Lake implements include choppers and adzes that are triangular in cross-section, thick scraper-planes, and lanceolate points that are not as well made as Agate Basin points; but there are no side-notched points. Eventually Shield people and styles dominated most of the Canadian Precambrian Shield, including all regions

Plate 34. Shield Implements from the Keewatin The notched spearheads, an endscraper (bottom right) and a knife blade (top centre) are characteristic tools of the Shield culture in the Keewatin District. The longest piece (top right), which lacks its base, may have been a combination lance and knife blade. Also present among Shield tools, but not illustrated, are leaf-shaped points and stone wedges. The spearhead at top left is 11 cm long.

around Hudson Bay except the most northerly reaches and parts of the coast that were barely habitable. This Shield homeland, though remote and harsh, provided an adequate-or-better level of subsistence through exploitation of the caribou herds of the southern Keewatin and northernmost Manitoba.

The Shield culture seems to have been an indigenous development in the Subarctic, not an import from the south. However, its possession of side-notched points indicates that it participated in a process of continent-wide technological change, possibly owing to style introductions from the eastern woodlands. Shield country was suited to a mixed hunting and fishing way of life, with emphasis on caribou hunting. Life for some continued to be the same as during past millennia, though styles of tools changed. Yet, Shield people adapted to a broader range of environmental conditions and colonized new areas. Some prehistorians believe that the Shield culture was the first to become fully adapted to permanent occupation of the boreal forest in the Shield region. At the time, the climate was warmer than it is at present, and the transition from forest to tundra lay farther north.

Shield people stayed east of the Subarctic's biggest lakes— Great Bear, Great Slave, Athabasca and Winnipeg. Rarely did they wander west of the Thelon River in the eastern Mackenzie District. Their main expansion was eastward into lands late to be freed of lingering ice, the Tyrrell Sea, and glacial lakes. Perhaps lands to the west were already securely occupied by others. The Shield culture may have been so well adapted to the region after which it was named that the people preferred to stay there, and when they ventured out, failed to succeed in displacing others. By 4 200 years ago, the Shield people had spread across northern Ontario and Quebec to the interior of Labrador, which they reached by about 3 500 years ago. In the north, however, they were supplanted by Palaeo-Eskimos about 3 400 years ago. Elsewhere, the Shield culture continued to develop, and later phased into the Laurel culture, when most of the bands adopted pottery. But that story comes later. The adaptability and expansive energy of the Shield culture suggests that, on the whole, the people were doing better than merely eking out a subsistence-level existence in the forest.

Common Shield implements include endscrapers and side-scrapers. Double-edged knives flaked on both faces were also common, as were unifacial tools. Over time the numerous lanceolate points were gradually replaced by side-notched points in both short and very long forms. Other implements include stone wedges and bar-shaped slate whetstones. The whetstones might have been used for finishing bone tools, none of which have been recovered. More-southerly Shield groups, including those living between Lake Winnipeg and the north shore of Lake Superior, beat implements from native copper and used adzes ground to an edge at the bit end. Cultural enrichment among these southern bands can be credited to trade or other forms of contact with different, richer cultures.

Direct recovery of information on the Shield culture is limited largely to these implements and to a few shelter remains, but considerable information on lifeways, such as the use of canoes and snowshoes, can be inferred from the environment and other characteristics of the region to which Shield people had adapted. Late Shield houses once overlooked the Thelon River in the Keewatin District. Two were recognized through the wealth of artifacts scattered over their shallow, oval-shaped floor depressions. In one, a simple hearth was located off-centre, while in the very middle of the 3-by-4.5-metre structure was a small pit lined with stone slabs. Poles probably supported a hide-covered structure, though no trace of them was recovered. A ring of stone weights that would have held down the edge of a hide cover outlined one shelter floor.

Occasional finds of Plains-style notched points document influence or incursions from the south that began about 5 000 years ago. These are too late to be responsible for the introduction of notched points into the Subarctic, and people living north of the southern fringe were probably little influenced by Plains culture.

At first, the Shield people had no neighbours to the north. In the North-Central Area, the coast of the Arctic Ocean and the islands beyond lay vacant—inhospitable and unmanageable by techniques adapted to the forest and forest-tundra edge. This changed about 4 200 years ago, when Palaeo-Eskimos swept eastwards. However, there is no clear evidence of any contact between these ancestral Eskimos and the Indians of the Canadian Subarctic.

Plate 35. Selected Tools of the Palaeo-Eskimos From the North-Central Area are a burin (bottom right); an endscraper to its left; above that a teardrop-shaped knife; unidentified objects with corner spurs (top right) and fish-like shape (second from left); a probable stemmed knife 7.6 cm long (top left); two small arrow tips (bottom left), one bipointed; and a small ulu in the top row.

A Palaeo-Eskimo Interlude

A long period of climatic cooling set in 4 000 years ago, and lasted for a millennium. The treeline and edge of the Barrens shifted southwards, as did the caribou's winter range in the forest. Far to the south the boreal forest moved in concert, reaching the southern end of Lake Winnipeg some time before 3 500 years ago. The people of the Shield also moved south to escape the increasingly harsh conditions in the north. But as the Barren Grounds expanded, a people able to cope with that environment arrived there. These were Palaeo-Eskimos, also known as the Pre-Dorset culture.

The Pre-Dorset people not only occupied the Barrens, but penetrated into the forests of the interior as far south as Lake Athabasca. In the wooded Mackenzie River valley, their artifacts have been found along the Great Bear River, but they did not range as far south in the valley as they did in the North-Central Area. This was probably because the distribution and migration of caribou herds differed between the two areas, and because other people occupied the forest lands. Whether the territories that the Palaeo-Eskimos occupied had already been abandoned or whether they ousted the Indian inhabitants has not been determined conclusively. The youngest acceptable radiocarbon date of a Shield culture artifact from the Barren Lands is about 3 600 to 3 700 years old. Thus far, the earliest radiocarbon dates from the succeeding Palaeo-Eskimo sites in the interior are about 3 200 to 3 300 years old (plus a single date of 3 500 years from the forest zone). This dating suggests that the two populations did not meet—that the Indians had withdrawn, leaving the land unoccupied.

Camp traces of the inland Pre-Dorset generally consist of stone tools scattered around a hearth marked by a cluster of fire-cracked rocks. There may be several hearths at a single site, each indicating the shelter of one of the families that travelled and camped together as a small band. Traces of the shelter itself are rare, but a site with dwelling floors has been found near Churchill, Manitoba. Frequently, camp remains and artifacts are exposed to view, making excavation unnecessary. The reason is the Palaeo-Eskimo penchant for camping on sandy ground, later swept free of soil and vegetation by the wind.

Most Palaeo-Eskimo tools are highly distinctive compared to those of other Subarctic cultures. They stand out in style, the care with which they were fashioned, their generally small size, and the raw materials of which they were made. Although Palaeo-Eskimos had microblades, any relation with microblade users in the northwestern Subarctic is remote and indirect. The Palaeo-Eskimos had many skills not previously developed in the Far North, including hunting on the sea and on the sea ice for seals and other sea mammals. They used the bow and arrow at a time when Indians in the Subarctic evidently did not. Late Palaeo-Eskimos in the Yukon and Alaska made ceramic pots using techniques derived from Siberia. Occasionally, too, they ground implements out of slate and even beat native copper nuggets into tools—techniques that later would become commonplace in parts of the Subarctic. However, it is not known whether there was any interaction between the peoples of the boreal forest and the Arctic newcomers, as no evidence of such contact or of cultural borrowing has been recovered.

The Bow and Arrow

The first firm evidence that northern Indians used the bow and arrow is relatively late. Now might be the time to explore this subject, before we enter the period during which use of the bow and arrow can be established.

Early Indians hunted primarily with spears, hurled by hand or with the help of a throwing device, called an *atlatl*, that served as an extension of the arm. They also used jabbing lances, snares, traps, possibly fishing harpoons and nets, and structures for driving and capturing game animals. The adoption of the bow and arrow has been inferred from a decrease that occurred in the width and thickness of stone points. This decrease was especially pronounced at the base, or stem, which slipped into the hafting groove of the weapon's shaft; this shaft was only slightly thicker than that of the modern arrow. Features of the stem, including size, indicate that most Subarctic peoples began to use bows and arrows only a few centuries ago. That is later than when archery was adopted elsewhere on the continent. In Chapter 7, we will see that in the Eastern Area, for example, the Laurel people were using the bow and arrow through the last few centuries B.C.

Nevertheless, doubts remain as to whether the features of stone points are reliable guides for identifying them as either arrow or spear points. In the Western Subarctic in late-prehistoric times, arrowheads were usually made from bone and antler, and some, locally, were hammered out of native copper. Stone points were rarely used, and when they were, most took the form of blades mounted at the tips of bone or antler arrowheads. As bone and antler have a poor preservation record in the Subarctic, it may be premature to assume that the absence in the earlier archaeological sites of points made of those materials indicates that the bow and arrow was not yet in use. For these reasons, it is difficult to determine how widely the bow and arrow was used in the Western Subarctic or when it was first adopted.

6. The Later Prehistory of the North-Central Area
(2 600 Years Ago to Historical Times)

After the Palaeo-Eskimos, the Taltheilei

The Early Phase

Within a few centuries of their arrival in the Subarctic, the Palaeo-Eskimos returned north, and Indians reappeared in the interior Keewatin District, the eastern Mackenzie District, and northernmost Saskatchewan and Manitoba. They were the Taltheilei (taal-tee-lee) people, named for the Taltheilei Narrows at Great Slave Lake, where one of their campsites has been found. The withdrawal of the Palaeo-Eskimos and the arrival of the Taltheilei people may be linked with a reversion to earlier climatic conditions, resulting in a modest warming and the northward return of the forest. The environment became similar to that in the region today.

The earliest Taltheilei sites, dating as far back as about 2 600 years ago, have been found thus far in a limited area on the Barrens and in the northern transitional forest of the Thelon and Dubawnt drainage. The new arrivals occupied lands vacated by the Palaeo-Eskimos, but we do not know whether they forced the Palaeo-Eskimos out, or whether they simply rediscovered the caribou-hunting potential of an area that they found vacant. There is a gap between the latest radiocarbon dates for the Palaeo-Eskimos and the earliest dates for their successors. Since the Indians did not have immediate antecedents in the area, and there is no evidence that they had had contact with the Palaeo-Eskimos, the earliest Taltheilei people must have moved in from elsewhere. Taltheilei origins have yet to be traced. There is circumstantial evidence that they spoke a Northern Athapaskan language, and that this language originated among Northern Archaic people in the northern British Columbia-southern Yukon region. Possibly the earliest Taltheilei came from the same far-western area, but there is no hint of such ancestry in the earliest Taltheilei tools.

Among their enigmatic tools are elongate spear points that changed in style through time. Other characteristic implements were circular hide-scraping tablets (chithos); thick, narrow adzes with ground bits; slate whetstones; endscrapers; pointed and semilunar side-hafted knives; and peculiar toothed, or denticulate, flakes. All were made of stone. Many of these implements are similar to others already in wide use in the Subarctic, and whose use continued to

1 Neck
2 Caribou Hill
3 Duck Lake Narrows
4 Black Lake
5 Charlot River
6 Big Bay
7 Peace Point
8 Karpinsky
9 Caribou Hills sites
10 Windy Bay
11 Mountain Lake
12 Migod
13 Aberdeen
14 Thelon River sites
15 Hennessy
16 Waldron River
17 Taltheilei (type site)
18 Aylmer Lake sites
19 Sites north of
    Yellowknife
20 Frank Channel
21 Fisherman Lake &
    Pointed Mountain
22 Northeastern Great
    Bear Lake
23 Bloody Falls
24 South shore, Lake
    Athabasca

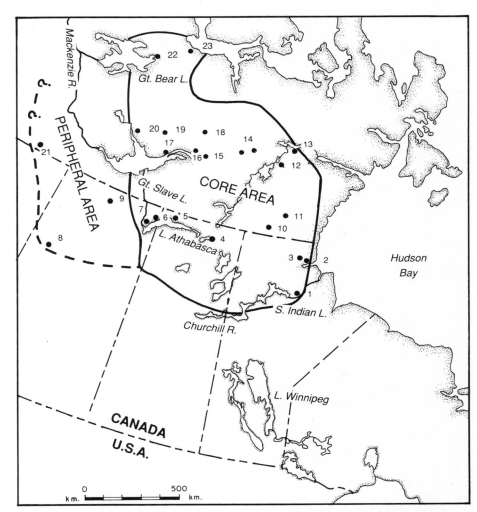

Map 9. Distribution of the Taltheilei Culture This map of the North-Central Area and adjacent lands shows the extent of the Taltheilei tradition and its major archaeological sites from 2 500 years ago to historical times.

Plate 37. Knives and Lances This selection of biface knife and lance blades, from middle to late prehistory, are from the Yukon, the Mackenzie River Valley and Great Bear Lake. The 13.2-cm-long knife blade at lower left has been sharpened on the right edge only.

Plate 36. Lance Blade This fine specimen, 21.2 cm long, was found at Fond du Lac on the eastern reach of Lake Athabasca by the geologist Robert Bell in 1882. This probable Taltheilei tool was one of the earliest items from present northern Saskatchewan to be deposited in the Canadian Museum of Civilization collections. It would be another ninety years before an archaeologist first excavated a site at Lake Athabasca.

historical times. By A.D. 100, Taltheilei occupation had spread to a broad region extending eastwards from Great Bear and Great Slave lakes, Lake Athabasca and northern Alberta. It did not quite reach the Arctic Ocean and Hudson Bay at that time.

The Middle Phase

By the beginning of its Middle phase, the Taltheilei tradition had expanded throughout the northern interior east of the Mackenzie River, including northern Alberta and Manitoba south to Southern Indian Lake. Camps were within sight of the Arctic Ocean at Bloody Falls on the Coppermine River, and approached Hudson Bay near Churchill, Manitoba. The Middle Taltheilei phase extended from about 2 000 to 1 000 years ago, and is distinguished by its lanceolate and square-stemmed spear points. Some of these points are similar in outline to Agate Basin Plano points that are thousands of years older. Other points are small, and may have been used on arrows. Some Middle Taltheilei artifacts are similar to Early-phase tools. Prominent are large double-edged knife and lance blades, ground smooth on the base edges for hafting, and ovoid knives that lack distinct butt and tip ends. The latter type was probably held along one side and used in the manner of an Eskimo semilunar knife, or ulu.

To Historical Times

The Late Taltheilei tradition began about 1 000 years ago and continued into the nineteenth century, when it emerged as a regional Dene or Athapaskan culture. Evidently, most late sites were occupied by ancestral Chipewyan Athapaskans. Late Taltheilei campsites are also found in the territory of the extinct Yellowknives and in the early-historical homeland of the Beaver Athapaskans. Other Taltheilei sites lie within the recent hunting range of the Hare and Dogrib Dene around Great Bear Lake and Great Slave Lake. Knowledge of the prehistory of the Mackenzie River valley is too fragmented to permit close comparison with the Taltheilei tradition; the Slavey, Hare and eastern Kutchin (Loucheux) Athapaskans live there today. Both similarities and differences are apparent. The Athapaskan dialects spoken in the Mackenzie River valley, in Alberta and eastward are all closely related, with the exception of Kutchin, spoken near the Mackenzie Delta. They probably diverged only within the past few

Plate 38. Large Taltheilei Tools The two double-ended adze bits with flaked ends (top left) are distinctive tools of the Taltheilei tradition; they were probably used for felling trees and splitting wood. The two other adze-bit styles (top right and bottom, second from left) have a wide distribution, and were used for conventional shaping tasks. The three large flakes that are retouched or sharpened at the edges (centre, bottom left, and second from right at bottom) might have served as knives, especially for skinning or flensing large animals like caribou. At bottom right is a biface knife blade. The adze bit at top right is 12 cm long.

centuries, and may have a common prehistoric source in the language spoken by those responsible for the widespread Late Taltheilei phase. The earlier Taltheilei phases may represent Athapaskans at a time before the historical tribes and dialects east of the Cordillera had formed. Indeed, some of their predecessors, whose spear points and hide-scrapers we now find, may have become extinct through an almost random succession of tragic events, such as starvation, enemy raids, and the accidental deaths of too many women of child-bearing age. These unfortunates are doomed to eternal silence. Luckier bands absorbed the survivors, and their descendants are the people of the North we know today.

The Late Taltheilei phase is recognized through its notched spear and arrow points. These reappeared after a complete absence of notched points in the North-Central Area for more than 1 500 years. They may represent an attempt to copy prehistoric Cree styles or Plains points. Similarly, people living in the Mackenzie River valley and farther west could have provided models for Late Taltheilei notched points. Lanceolate points for tipping spears also continued to be made in late times. Copper implements, consisting of multipurpose prongs (for example, awls) and small knife blades, were now common. Only a few of the bone and antler tools and items of hunting equipment that Taltheilei people evidently used have been recovered. Distinctive chipped, arched adzes used for felling small trees and for heavy woodworking tasks were double-bitted. Most previous types of stone knives and scrapers continued in use.

Only hearths and cobble tent-weights have been identified from Middle and Late Taltheilei dwellings. Nevertheless, the brush shelters and skin tents, caribou-hunting surrounds and skin and birch-bark boats used in early historical times must have been known to Late Taltheilei people as well as to their antecedents. Cobbles from tent rings survive on a few late sites. Some are widely scattered; others are still arranged in circles, and in rare cases surround floors stained from occupation. Hearth traces, surrounded by clustered artifacts, are all that remain of most camps, but they allow us to envisage families cooking meat on skewer stakes stuck into the ground next to the fire, and women placing heated rocks into baskets to boil soup, the main beverage of ancient times. Sooty, fist-sized cobbles from this stone-boiling method of cooking have been found at old campsites.

Plate 39. Taltheilei Stone Points

The photograph displays a progression of stone points from the earliest styles to the latest types that were replaced by imported metal points and fire-arms. Beginning with the two narrow stemmed points, (top left), styles changed to broader stemmed spearheads, to lanceolate forms in middle Taltheilei times (the first three in the middle row), to side-notched points in later times (two each at middle right and bottom left), and to small arrow tips during late times. Spearhead at upper right is 9.2 cm long.

Men sitting nearby making tools may be responsible for the broken implements or clusters of stone chips. In this vision are a conical skin tent or brush shelters, and in the background a rack of equipment. Some hearths were probably inside the shelters, which in summer provided an escape from the clouds of mosquitoes and biting flies. What must have been roasting hearths were used near Great Slave Lake. Their traces consist of piles of fire-cracked cobbles that had been heated, probably in a pit. Chunks of meat would have been placed on the hot cobbles, covered with leaves, sealed with turf, and left for several hours to roast.

Late Taltheilei people, like their Middle predecessors, extended south to the Churchill River in Saskatchewan and Manitoba, and, judging from some point finds, into northern Alberta. Parts of this area were also utilized by ancestral Cree. Perhaps the hunting ranges of these two peoples overlapped, or one or the other occupied the over-lapping territory during different periods. They might have avoided contact to lessen the chance of conflict, but at times might have sought one another out for purposes of trade. Shifts in tribal territories and major linguistic boundaries occurred all through the Subarctic during both prehistoric and historical times. During the early fur-trade period, warring Cree expanded their trapping territories to the north and west, and tried to exclude Athapaskans, especially the Chipewyan and Beaver, from direct contact with European traders. Later, the Cree were weakened by smallpox, and, concurrently, the Chipewyan became increasingly involved in fur trapping. This combination of factors resulted in the partial withdrawal of the Cree southwards, the retreat of the Chipewyan from the Barren Grounds, and, as part of a chain reaction, the movement of Eskimos deep into the Barrens and into former Chipewyan territory.

Influences from the South

From far below Latitude 60, Plains people occasionally made north-ward incursions into the coniferous and mixed-wood forests, where they may have interacted with their Subarctic neighbours. Artifacts pointing to this activity include distinctive varieties of notched and stemmed points, each identified with an archaeological phase on the Plains. They range in age from 5 000 years ago or earlier to about 600 years ago. It is doubtful, though, that there was any substantial

Plate 40. Copper Technology and Implements The large copper nugget from the southwestern Yukon has been pounded at one end to detach smaller pieces. Unfinished items, from the Northwestern and North-Central areas, are copper rolled and beaten into a bar and a partially flattened nugget (top left). Finished tools include four sharp implements formed from bars, one a hook in its bone shank (bottom right) and another possibly an awl (below nugget); a bipointed fish gorge (second from bottom right); three small stemmed knives formed from pounded sheet copper, shown above the back-hafted, single-edged knife blade with hole to assist in hafting; and two stemmed arrowheads (third from left above blade and third from bottom right). Ornaments and large daggers were also crafted from native copper, though not shown here. The knife blade at lower left is 12 cm long.

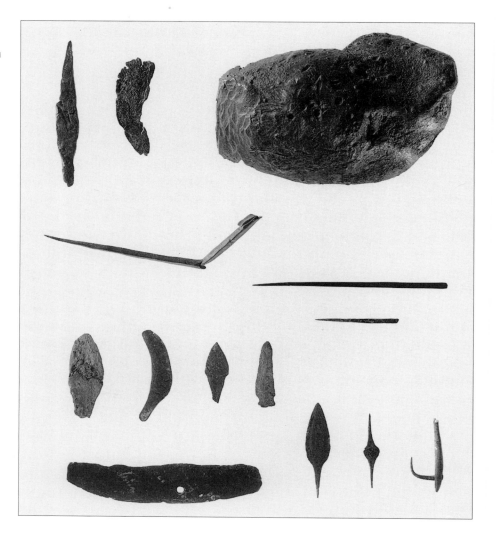

and persistent occupation of the Subarctic by Plains people. The Plains lifestyle, which focused on the buffalo hunt, was not the boreal-forest lifeway, even though Subarctic peoples hunted wood bison throughout much of northern Alberta, in parts of northern Saskatchewan, and in the southern Mackenzie District. Only rarely did Plains excursions go north of the mixed-wood forest or north of the Churchill River and its tributaries.

Notched points found farther north sometimes resemble Plains points. Regional experts claim that correspondences are inexact. Imprecise copying by the northerners or even sheer coincidence may be responsible. Nevertheless, a Plains-related people may have drifted northwards into the Mackenzie River valley about 1 000 years ago. Evidence for this consists of numerous Prairie side-notched points, a style dated to 1 300–600 years ago in the south. The brief summers in the valley are warm, there are no major topographical barriers between the valley and the Plains, and the fast current of the major rivers could have carried people northwards. But what language did they speak? We are reasonably certain that by this time, some 1 000 years ago, Athapaskan speakers occupied the Mackenzie River valley. Perhaps they also occupied the southern transitional forest, as many Athapaskan speakers do today. Language, then, would have been no barrier to population movements.

Coppersmiths of the North

A fascinating aspect of prehistoric technology is the use of metals by people with a Stone Age way of life. Nearly 2 000 years ago, small bits of smelted iron were traded across the Bering Strait into Alaska, enabling people to improve their cutting and carving tools. But this metal rarely reached the interior of the continent. Instead, Subarctic peoples developed techniques for working the more abundant native copper, which is found in nature in its metallic state.

The primary method of working copper was to hammer it into thin, flat sheets. The sheets were then cut into different shapes, which were sharpened at the edges to make tools, such as thin, semilunar knife blades, or were rolled to make conical "tinkler" ornaments and tubular beads. If a sturdier object was wanted, a sheet was folded over on itself, or stacked on one or more other sheets,

Plate 41. Copper Technology These four steps were followed to fashion copper tools in the North-Central and Northwestern areas. (Adapted from a diagram published in U. Franklin et al., 1981)

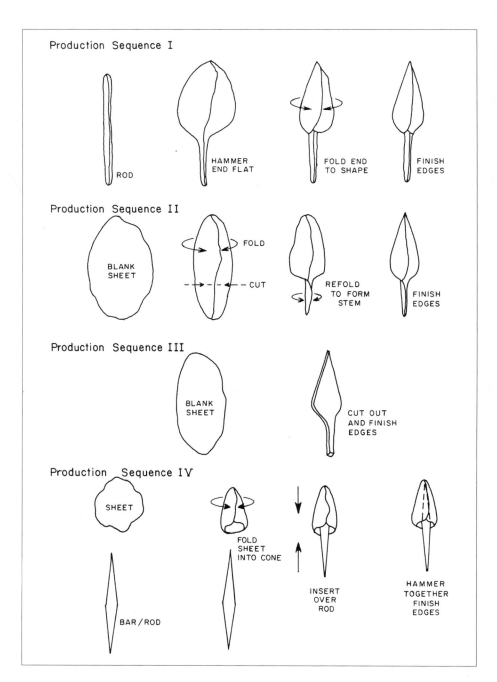

Production Sequence I

ROD

HAMMER
END FLAT

FOLD END
TO SHAPE

FINISH
EDGES

Production Sequence II

BLANK
SHEET

FOLD

CUT

REFOLD
TO FORM
STEM

FINISH
EDGES

Production Sequence III

BLANK
SHEET

CUT OUT
AND FINISH
EDGES

Production Sequence IV

SHEET

BAR/ROD

FOLD
SHEET
INTO CONE

INSERT
OVER
ROD

HAMMER
TOGETHER
FINISH
EDGES

and hammered to weld the layers together. This technique was developed because the raw material was rarely available in large pieces. Much later, Indians used the same technique to build up European sheet-copper into thicker stock. But pounding makes copper hard and brittle. If the sheets became too brittle, they could not be folded without breaking. The solution, known to blacksmiths as annealing, was to heat the copper to resoften it. Microscopical examination of copper artifacts done at the University of Toronto established that, in fact, Native-made copper artifacts were annealed. However, the separation of layers in some specimens indicates that the processing was sometimes imperfect. Bars formed by folding were sharpened to a point at one end, and bent if necessary, to make various prongs, hooks, gaffs, awls and ornaments; or they were further hammered into other implements, as described next.

Knives and arrow points with long stems to be inserted into hafts are both abundant. These were made in three ways: 1) One end of a bar was flattened and shaped to form the blade, and the rest of the bar served as the stem. 2) A sheet was rolled into a cone, which was hammered flat over the end of a bar and shaped into a blade; the cone and bar, now firmly united, formed the blade and stem respectively. 3) One end of a sheet was folded to form the stem by using the same technique used to make a bar, while the other, flat end was trimmed and sharpened into a blade.

This basic technology was used throughout the North, though the items produced differed from one area to another. The major areas where copper tools were made radiated outwards from the native-copper sources. One encompassed the Mackenzie District north of Great Slave Lake and along the Arctic coast. There, copper tools were made by both Indians and Eskimos, especially the Yellowknife Athapaskans and the Copper Eskimos, whose names reflect this technology. Farther to the west, several Athapaskan groups of the western Yukon and eastern Alaska made a variety of copper tools, utilizing material from sources on both flanks of the Wrangell Mountains. Other western Athapaskan tribes, coastal Pacific Eskimos and West Coast Indians who lived farther from this source also had copper tools, which they obtained through trade or produced themselves from traded raw metal. Another major source area was along the shores of Lake Superior, from which some copper reached the ancestral Cree and Ojibwa of Manitoba and Ontario.

Given the similarities in metal-smithing techniques between regions, northern copper-working probably developed in one area first and then spread to others. Whereas the simple technique of beating copper could have been reinvented by different peoples over and over again, the complete process of copper-working is more complex. The technique of annealing cannot be perceived through visual or manual examination of the product; thus, its spread must have occurred through learning from others rather than repeated instances of isolated development. Nevertheless, the possibility remains that boreal-forest people had long been aware of the effects of treating materials by heat, through the conceptually related process of heating pieces of chert and quartzite to make them more flakable. Heat treatment of stone was widespread in North America, but we lack information on its use in the Subarctic. Additional circumstantial evidence suggesting diffusion after a major technological breakthrough, probably annealing, is provided by the widespread late rise to popularity of copper-working among Athapaskans and Eskimos during the second millennium A.D. However, there is no evidence to suggest that copper-working in the North is related to that in the Great Lakes region. There may have been more than one North American origin.

Life in the Transitional Forest Zone and on the Barrens

In historical times, the traditional Chipewyan Athapaskan inhabitants of the central region moved southwards, farther into the forest, and the Caribou Eskimo entered the interior Barren Lands. By the time ethnologists visited them, the Chipewyan had been interacting with white traders for more than two centuries. Their lifeways had changed, and much traditional knowledge had been lost. Nevertheless, the narratives of early explorers convey the essence of the Indians' earlier way of life. Samuel Hearne's *A Journey from Prince of Wales's Fort in Hudson's Bay to the Northern Ocean . . . in the Years 1769, 1770, 1771 & 1772* and Richard King's later *Narrative of a Journey to the Shores of the Arctic Ocean, in 1833, 1834 and 1835* are quoted extensively here to provide early personal observations. Given the highly focused life of the people of tundra and boreal forest, almost totally dependent on caribou, Hearne and King may have witnessed virtually the same Native subsistence patterns as had prevailed in earlier times.

Caribou was the key resource, and caribou hunting the key activity. Most prehistoric tools from the region are related to the caribou hunt, to butchering the animals, and to processing their hides, or are the tools required to produce equipment used in hunting, travelling and camping. According to King:

> The rein-deer supplies the Chipewyans, Copper Indians, Dog Ribs, and Hare Indians with food, who would be totally unable to inhabit their barren lands were it not for the immense herds of this deer that exist there. Of the horns they form their fish-spears and hooks; and . . . ice-chisels and various other utensils were made of them.
>
> . . . [Following a description of skin-dressing:] The skins thus dressed are used as winter clothing; and, by sewing sixty or seventy together, will make a covering for a tent sufficient for the residence of a large family. The undressed hide, after the hair is taken off, is cut into thongs of various thickness, which are twisted into deer-snares, bow-strings, net-lines, and, in fact, supply all the purposes of rope. The finer thongs are used in the manufacture of fishing-nets, or in making snow-shoes; while the tendons of the dorsal muscles are split into fine and excellent sewing thread. . . .
>
> . . . Every part of the animal is consumed, even to the contents of the stomach. . . . By collecting the blood and boiling it, they also form a very rich soup, which is considered a dainty. When all the soft parts are consumed, the bones are pounded small, and a large quantity of marrow is extracted from them by boiling, which is used in making the better kinds of the mixture of dried meat and fat, termed pemmican (King 1836: 152–54).

The calendar might appear overly busy with caribou hunts, but not everyone was positioned to pursue every hunt. Sometimes, too, a hunt failed. And bad weather was often a hazard. A severe, prolonged winter or a cold, rainy summer, when people were on the Barrens, thwarted nearly every kind of activity and made life a misery.

Caribou Spring

Every spring the caribou return northwards after wintering in the forest. The people have already moved north, and are waiting to drive the caribou between lines of cairns built to resemble hunters, which will channel deer to places where they can be killed easily with short-range spears.

But before people ventured out of the forest, they had to prepare for the months on the Barrens. Samuel Hearne described these preparations:

> Agreeably to the Indians' proposals we remained at Thelewey-aza-yeth [on the Thlewiaza River] ten days [in early April]; during which time my companions were busily employed . . . in preparing small staves of birch-wood. . . . These served as tent-poles while on the barren ground. . . . Birch-rind [bark], together with timbers and other wood-work for building canoes, were also another object of the Indian's attention . . . but as the canoes were not to be set up till our arrival at Clowey . . . all the wood-work was reduced to its proper size, for the sake of making it light for carriage.
>
> . . . Those vessels . . . though very slight and simple in their construction, are nevertheless the best that could possibly be contrived for the use of those poor people, who are frequently obliged to carry them a hundred, and sometimes a hundred and fifty miles at a time, without having occasion to put them into the water. Indeed, the chief use of these canoes is to ferry over unfordable rivers; though sometimes . . . they are of great service in killing deer . . . swans, geese, ducks, etc. (Hearne 1795: 87–88, 96–97).

Native women were indispensible in the carrying out of all these tasks, but their contribution was taken for granted and apparently poorly rewarded. Hearne recounts what Motonabbee, a Chipewyan, told him about the hard role and low status of women in the region:

> Said he, when all the men are heavy laden, they can neither hunt nor travel to any considerable distance; and in case they meet with success in hunting, who is to carry the produce of their labour? Women . . . were made for labour; one of them can carry, or haul, as much as two men can do. They also pitch our tents, make and mend our clothing, keep us warm at night; and, in fact, there is no such thing as travelling any considerable distance . . . in this country, without their assistance. Women . . . though they do every thing, are maintained at a trifling expense; for as they always stand cook, the very licking of their fingers in scarce times is sufficient for their subsistence (Hearne 1795: 55).

Plate 42. A Pack Dog on the Barrens, 1915 Even tent poles had to be taken along when moving north into the treeless Barren Grounds. Pack dogs were probably important to Native peoples in prehistoric times as they were later. One or two dogs could also be hitched to a small sled or toboggan, but dog traction did not become highly developed in the northwestern interior until after the gold rushes of the 1890s. (Photograph by G. H. Wilkins, CMC neg. 50974)

Summer

The caribou continue their migration through calving, and disperse on reaching the Barrens. As they funnel across rivers and lakes at accustomed crossings, many families gather there, and the hunt continues. Caribou are lanced in the water from the canoes that have been hauled north, or are ambushed on land as they come ashore. The summer caribou hunt on the Barrens is also an important time for families to renew social contacts with others who went their separate ways in the forest during the past year.

> In a few days, many others joined us from different quarters; so that by the thirtieth of July [1770] we had in all above seventy tents, which did not contain less than six hundred persons. . . . In the morning, when we began to move, the whole ground . . . seemed to be alive, with men, women, children, and dogs. Though the land was entirely barren . . . yet the deer were so numerous that the Indians not only killed as many as were sufficient for our large number, but often several merely for the skins, marrow, etc. (Hearne 1795: 40).

Each year, arctic char return to the swift northern rivers to spawn, and may have been speared at some localities. Historical Natives placed boulder weirs across the streams to impede the chars' progress, and then killed them with pronged spears. In any case, if there was fishing on the Barrens in prehistoric times, it would have been subordinate to caribou hunting, as would searching for bird's eggs and pursuing the abundant waterfowl. Living on the Barren Grounds demanded a lot of walking, backpacking, and moving from place to place, at the right time, for hunting and fishing. People may have made use of the occasional pack dog, in view of the widespread domestication of dogs in North America since Late Palaeo-Indian times.

In August, families began to return southwards. Some whose winter camps were near the lush blueberry patches of the forest edge picked and stored large quantities of them in pits. Those who lived deeper in the forest could only swell their bellies with fruit and move on.

Plate 43. An Early-Historical Caribou Fence Located on the eastern side of Great Bear Lake near Hornby Bay, this fence is positioned at a stream crossing above a gorge that directed caribou into the fence wings, which led into several corrals. Snares may have been set in the corrals, but most details of the fence have been lost to decay. Compare with the Kutchin caribou fence shown in Plate 29.

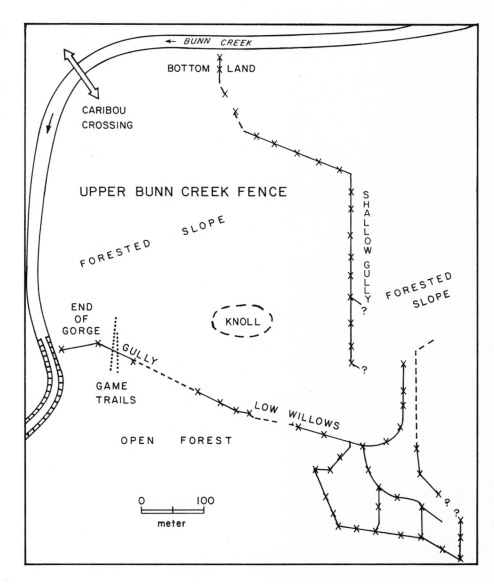

← BUNN CREEK

BOTTOM LAND

CARIBOU CROSSING

UPPER BUNN CREEK FENCE

FORESTED SLOPE

SHALLOW GULLY

FORESTED SLOPE

KNOLL

END OF GORGE

GULLY

GAME TRAILS

LOW WILLOWS

OPEN FOREST

0   100
meter

Autumn and Winter

The Barrens are a disagreeable place to be when cold, moist air and snow squalls blow in from the Arctic Ocean. September brings the first hard frosts, driving both hunter and caribou south towards the forest. Thus, autumn is the time for making a concentrated effort to intercept the caribou, both at crossing points and at the surrounds, or pounds. Their hides—now free of the holes made by warble-fly larvae and with pelage of optimum length and durability—are ideal for shelter covers and clothing. The water-crossing points are predictable, as caribou have evidently used many of the same ones for millennia. At these crossings, archaeologists almost invariably find prehistoric sites, some of which have been occupied by various peoples through thousands of years.

Caribou surrounds have probably been built since ancient times in the Subarctic, though the evidence is circumstantial. Samuel Hearne described their construction and operation in the eighteenth century:

> Indians . . . pitch their tent on or near to an eminence that affords a commanding prospect of the path leading to the pound; and when they see any deer going that way, men, women, and children walk along the lake or river-side under cover of the woods, till they get behind them, then step forth to open view, and proceed towards the pound in the form of a crescent. The poor timorous deer finding themselves pursued, and at this same time taking the two rows of brushy poles to be two ranks of people stationed to prevent their passing on either side, run straight forward in the path till they get into the pound. The Indians then close in, and block up the entrance with some brushy trees. . . . The deer being thus enclosed, the women and children walk round the pound, to prevent them from breaking or jumping over the fence, while the men are employed spearing such as are entangled in the snares, and shooting with bows and arrows those which remain loose in the pound (Hearne 1795: 79–80).

Some people spent all winter close to the surround, neither on the Barrens nor wholly in the forest, living off its proceeds until spring, when in Hearne's words (p. 80), "both the deer and Indians draw out to the Eastward, on the ground which is entirely barren." At the beginning of March 1770, he visited some Indians who had been living there in a large tent "from the beginning of Winter, and had found a

Plate 44. "Whatzit," Taltheilei Culture An unidentified serrated implement, 6.5 cm long, from the Barren Grounds

plentiful subsistence by catching deer in a pound" (p.78). Many ancient sites may have been associated with caribou pounds, which, being made of perishable materials, have disappeared without a trace. Some sites have been found where the topography, such as glacial ridges or eskers, may have been enlisted to channel caribou to water crossings or to pounds.

Other families dispersed into the forest. Hearne commented on these variations in winter domicile by noting that the ease of obtaining subsistence at the pound was well adapted to the needs of the old and infirm, but did not provide the young and active with the opportunity to take fur-bearing animals, which inhabit the forest.

A few people may have stayed year-round on the Barrens, an unlikely but not impossible alternative to the gruelling seasonal migrations. Winter life there in a skin shelter would have been unpleasant without wood for fuel and the forest to break the Arctic winds. Sites of late-prehistoric age provide evidence that large camps sheltered aggregations of people on the Barrens and that more-numerous smaller camps were dispersed throughout the transitional forest zone. Thus, archaeological finds support the pattern that Hearne describes, of large summer camps on the Barrens and winter dispersal into the forest, paralleling the movements of the caribou.

Just as they had made special preparations for summering on the Barrens, those who wintered deep in the forest also had to prepare for their return.

> Deer at this time [late September] being very plentiful, and the few woods we met with affording tent-poles and firing [fuel], the Indians proposed to remain where we were some time, in order to dress skins, and provide our Winter clothing; also to make snow-shoes and temporary sledges, as well as to prepare a large quantity of dried meat and fat to carry with us (Hearne 1795: 204).

In the forest, the people continued hunting for dispersed caribou, moose, and in some areas bison, though with mixed success. They set nets under the ice in places where fish remained available during winter months and where currents kept the ice thin. Such localities, which were well known and are remembered today, often show evidence of past occupation. Small game, such as hare and ptarmigan, and animals that today are regarded primarily as furbearers, were taken with deadfall traps and snares, and hunters searched for hibernating black bears. During the coldest, darkest days, people remained inside their shelters much of the time. As spring arrived, they moved out towards the edge of the forest and the Barrens, once more launched on their unremitting pursuit of a basic level of subsistence.

This chapter completes our review of the North-Central and North-western areas, which together constitute most of the region termed by ethnographers the "Western Subarctic," a region they identify with the distribution of Northern Athapaskan speakers in historical times. There remains to be examined a broad belt, identified historically with Cree speakers, along the southern flank of the North-Central Area. This belt is a western extension of the ethnographer's "Eastern Subarctic."

7. The Eastern Area from Early to Historical Times

In delineating the Eastern Area discussed in this chapter, we have set an arbitrary eastern boundary that eliminates Quebec and all but the western part of northern Ontario (see Map 1). The environment, lifeways, prehistoric cultures, and historical tribes described here were similar to those farther east, with some aspects becoming gradually more complex closer to the Great Lakes and St. Lawrence River regions. Our Eastern Area may be regarded as a westward extension of the ethnographer's "Eastern Subarctic." Its early to middle prehistory is closely related to that of the eastern Mackenzie and Keewatin districts, as parts of both were occupied by peoples of the Northern Plano and Shield cultures. In later prehistoric times, however, this Eastern Area, or subarctic flank, became a distinctly separate entity.

The Deep-Forest Environment

In earlier chapters, we examined subsistence lifeways in the northwestern mountains and valleys, which drew on a variety of resources, in contrast to the dependence on caribou herds in the transitional forest zone and on the Barrens. The boreal forests of Saskatchewan, Manitoba and northwestern Ontario lack the topographical diversity of the Northwestern Area and its rich resources of salmon and upland game. In comparison with the North-Central Area, the Eastern Area has a much smaller tundra and transitional forest zone, but has a bordering parkland, or Plains transitional zone in the south. In fact, both the North-Central and Eastern areas lie primarily within the Precambrian Shield. The correlation of the physiography and vegetation with the rock formations of the Precambrian Shield is so close that geographers recognize a "Shield Subarctic" region. Our Eastern Area also includes part of the Hudson Bay Lowlands, whose features are open woodland, shrubland and tundra, and, to the west, the forested plains underlain by sedimentary rocks that extend beyond the Shield into Alberta. However, most of the Eastern Area is underlain by Shield rock and is characterized by sharply defined but small-scale topographical features. Innumerable lakes, ponds, streams, and varied patches of vegetation help break up the monotony of the boreal forest, as do the larger lakes and the wild rivers such as the Churchill and Nelson.

1   Pelican Falls
2   Quimet
3   Potato Island
4   Severn River sites
5   Grand Rapids
6   Clearwater Lake
7   Elk Island
8   Neck
9   SIL 54
10 South Indian Lake sites
11 McBride
12 Pelican Narrows
13 Montreal Lake sites
14 Buffalo Narrows
15 Reindeer Lake sites
16 Black Lake (mainly
    Taltheilei)
17 Peace Point
18 Hickson-Maribelli, rock
    paintings
19 Rock paintings

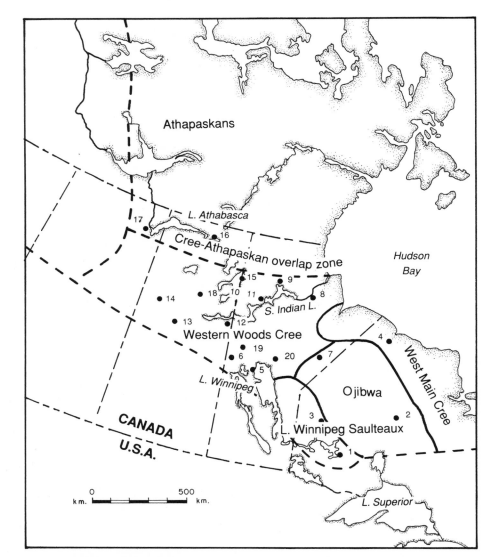

Map 10. The Eastern Area and Its Archaeological Sites, Showing Distribution of Indian Tribes in the Eighteenth and Nineteenth Centuries

Forest and tundra fires, usually started by lightening, often sweep the Subarctic, though their impact on prehistory is not known. In historical times, the diverse hunting areas and fishing sites of some bands have been burnt over by a succession of fires within a single generation, but rarely has an entire band area been rendered uninhabitable. In fact, burning even enhanced the habitat for game and the growth of berries. However, in the eastern Subarctic outside of the area described in this book, periodic burning of the mature white-spruce forest sometimes reached catastrophic proportions, with single fires devastating 20 000 square kilometres or more. They destroyed or displaced game, routed the human inhabitants, and may have resulted in the scattering or merging of peoples. Undoubtedly, people living outside the devastated zone had to share their hunting lands and resources with the displaced. As food resources in the forest are often meagre, conflict might have resulted. But precisely what did happen in prehistory under such circumstances is conjectural.

Deep-Forest Lifeways

The southeastern flank of the Subarctic was occupied in later prehistoric times mainly by the Cree Indians, and marginally, in parts of Ontario and southern Manitoba, also by Ojibwas. Influenced by contact with Europeans, they are thought to have adopted a fur-trade economy nearly three centuries ago. As this change occurred before explorers described the local cultures, it is particularly risky to extrapolate from later historical accounts to reconstruct life during prehistoric times. However, much information has been accumulated through archaeological research and interpretation. Most aspects of Subarctic subsistence were described in earlier chapters; here the characteristics peculiar to the Eastern Area are emphasized.

The Open Season

Because fishing was very important to survival, people settled on the shores of lakes, lake and river narrows, and the interconnecting network of streams during the ice-free season. There it was not only possible to catch whitefish, pike, lake trout and pickerel, but also to take moose, beaver, muskrat and other game close by. The most likely fishing method was to spear or dipnet fish trapped in a system of weirs, though gill nets may also have been used. The location of large archaeological sites at ideal fishing spots, such as narrows, indicates that people returned repeatedly to the same summer camps, many of which have been occupied, at least intermittently, for several thousand years.

During these warmer months, people were able to gather in larger groups than was possible in winter. Only two to five related families occupied a camp, but for a while every summer many camp groups of the same regional band would gather at certain localities. There people renewed personal bonds, exchanged news, planned partnerships for the coming winter, arranged marriages, traded crafts and local products, and celebrated with dances, ceremonies and athletic contests.

The Frozen Months

Early in winter, when the time came for the communal pursuit of woodland caribou, the hunters assembled at the surrounds. Individuals also tracked and killed moose, elk, bison, caribou, hibernating black bears and small game, according to the resources of the locality. Now that the weather had turned cold, a supply of meat could be stored for future use, and fish remained accessible until the ice grew too thick to chop through. To better pursue the hunting lifeway, people dispersed through the forest in small camp units, sometimes consisting of only one or two families living as a single household. Though both people and game were dispersed, travel over frozen bogs, lakes and streams was now easy. But to move through the forest, where snow fell soft and deep, the snowshoe would have been as essential as the canoe on lakes and rivers in the summer.

During the hard months of January and February, activity was limited to the immediate vicinity of camp. But before the spring thaw made travel impossible, people did get back to the pounds to take more caribou. Spring breakup brought rotten ice, soggy snow, flooded lowlands, and overflowing streams. When the water courses were open, the people headed for their summer camps and their band gatherings.

Late Palaeo-Indian and Shield Cultures

Late Palaeo-Indians, or Plano people, identifiable by their distinctive point styles, lived on the northern Plains, around the Great Lakes, in the transitional parkland zone along the southern fringe of the boreal forest, and on the Barren Grounds. Thus far, there is only sparse evidence of their having settled the boreal forest of Alberta, Saskatchewan and Manitoba, through which they reached the Barrens. The question that arises is whether people with a subsistence technology designed for the Plains and the transitional forest could have quickly developed the tools—such as snowshoes and bark canoes—that were necessary for life in the forested Shield Subarctic. Certainly, the people of the northern Plains knew how to cope with harsh winters and probably with travel on snow and water. Possibly, they quickly overcame the problems posed by forests and the Shield terrain, but we may never know whether they adapted successfully or how long it took.

The Shield culture—described in some detail in a previous chapter—is better represented in the Eastern Area than its Plano antecedents, especially in northern Manitoba. Some of the population may have arrived from farther north about 3 500 years ago, displaced by a worsening climate or driven out by Palaeo-Eskimos. By that time, Shield people or techniques had spread into northern Ontario and Quebec beyond the area covered by this volume. In northern and eastern Manitoba, the Shield culture persisted and underwent further development. From this base the Laurel culture developed.

Ceramic Cultures

The Laurel Culture

About 2 700 years ago, people of the Shield culture living in the Great Lakes area north of Lake Huron began learning how to make pottery. As pottery makers and users, they are designated as part of the Laurel culture, whose name comes from a site located in northern Minnesota. The adoption of pottery probably did not cause any major change in northern lifeways. But to the south and in the Eastern Woodlands, pottery-making was often characteristic of the settled way of life of horticultural societies. Therein lies its significance, even

Plate 45. Ceramics and Implements of the Laurel Culture The notched pebble at bottom left, probably a fishnet weight, is 8.9 cm long. A double-pointed copper awl is shown above the spear points, one of which (second from right) has been reshaped into an endscraper—an unusual conversion.

though horticulture and permanent settlements remained unfeasible in the Subarctic. The appearance of pottery there does provide prehistorians with a useful indicator for subdividing the long span of prehistory, especially as stone tools changed very little over time. Otherwise, the mixed hunting and fishing lifeway of Laurel people was undoubtedly similar to that of their local Shield ancestors who had occupied the same territory under similar environmental conditions.

Pottery never was adopted in some areas of North America. An explanation often heard is that people who moved camp frequently, or were seasonally nomadic, preferred more durable containers. But there are so many instances of pottery used by mobile peoples, including those of the southern boreal forest, that this explanation may not always apply. Analysis of the clay in pots found in two regions indicates that they had been transported from elsewhere in the Eastern Area. Evidently, a few people wanted clay pots badly enough to risk the possibility of breakage during their travels, and to take the trouble necessary to avoid it. Nevertheless, pottery's vulnerability to breakage under the conditions of life in the Subarctic may explain why ceramics were used by only a few groups, mainly those in close contact with pottery-using peoples to the south.

Laurel pottery originated far to the south and spread to Shield people along the north shore of Lake Huron about 2 700 years ago. The Laurel culture eventually extended over the entire south-central Subarctic region, consisting of parts of Quebec, Ontario, Manitoba and Saskatchewan, as well as northern Minnesota. Judging from the initial lack of change in other artifacts, pottery-making alone spread from one group to another at this time—a process referred to as *diffusion*. The Laurel phase reached Manitoba about 2 000 years ago, and arrived farther west later. It flourished until about 1 200 years ago, but may have persisted a few centuries longer north of Lake Winnipeg and in adjacent parts of Saskatchewan. There, the successors to Laurel were the Blackduck and Selkirk pottery styles.

Laurel pots were formed by the coiling technique, in which the clay, mixed with grit, was rolled into long rods, which were then coiled to build up the shape of the vessel. The surfaces were paddled to smooth out the grooves between coils and expand the vessel to its final size. Although some pots were left plain on the

Plate 46. Blackduck Ceramics and Implements In the bottom row are a side-scraper and five arrow tips, including an iron one from historical times (far right). The width of the rim sherd at upper left is 13 cm.

exterior, there is a great deal of variety in surface decoration. Before firing, the clay was impressed, jabbed and incised with small, toothed tools to make indented designs (referred to as "dragged-stamp" lines) and dot-like depressions that sometimes covered the whole upper half of the pot. Neither Laurel pottery nor any other type that appeared later in the region was burnished, glazed, or painted in polychrome designs, though some were painted red all over. Laurel vessels characteristically have cone-shaped bases, somewhat cylindrical or globular shapes, and slightly flaring rims.

Laurel people living farthest south and closest to the Great Lakes had a greater variety of goods, and probably a richer culture, than those who lived in the northern hinterland. They imported exotic trade goods from farther south and from the east. Those who lived around northeastern Lake Superior made tools from the native copper of that region, some of which reached more-distant Laurel people. Just north of Minnesota, people of the Laurel culture constructed earthen burial mounds over their dead, a practice presumably adopted from tribes living farther south. Otherwise, Laurel implements, such as those recovered from Manitoba, include the usual range of cutting and scraping tools, ground adze-bits, beaver-incisor carving-tool bits, bone awls, and corner-and side-notched arrow and spear points. Laurel people had the bow and arrow earlier than did the more northerly inhabitants of the Subarctic. Ontario finds indicate that some used additional bone and antler implements, among them toggling harpoon heads used for taking large fish. Judging from the distribution of Laurel people, they may have spoken an Algonquian tongue belonging to the language family that today includes the Cree and Ojibwa.

The Blackduck Tradition

About 1 200 years ago, pottery styles changed from Laurel to Blackduck, which persisted in parts of far-western Ontario and southern Manitoba until European contact. However, in the northern and western areas of its distribution, Blackduck was followed by another culture phase, Selkirk, thought to be ancestral Cree Indian. Blackduck is only minimally within the scope of this book. Its distribution overlaps that of Laurel, which may have contributed importantly to its development. Blackduck pots are usually globe-shaped and the

Plate 47. Probable Prehistoric and Early-Historical Cree Implements

These implements of the Selkirk phase include the Clearwater variety and specimens from northern Ontario. In the right-hand column are four projectile points and a small, stemmed, asymmetrical knife blade (centre), either Cree or Chipewyan. At top left is an adze blade with a ground and polished bit, and to the right of it are two biface knives. The 10.3-cm-long awl (bottom left) is formed from a large splinter of bird bone. Next to it are two bone tube-beads and two perforated snowshoe netting needles; such needles were used throughout the Subarctic, but are uncommon in archaeological deposits. Porcupine or beaver incisors, such as the one next to the snowshoe needles, were used as carving-tool bits in nearly every region of North America. Next to it is an unidentified cigar-shaped ground stone. Above the latter is a whetstone worn on the left edge, and to its left is a rough biface blade.

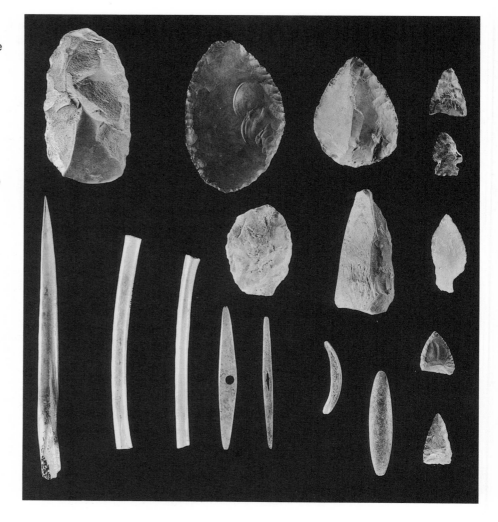

neck constricted, with a flaring rim; they are elaborately decorated with dot-like indentations and the impressions of a cord-wrapped tool, and occasionally bear a fabric-impressed design. The cord and fabric markings distinguish Blackduck pottery from Laurel.

A Blackduck population occupied part of Ontario west of Lake Superior, the region around and south of Lake Winnipeg, and northern Minnesota. However, the Blackduck style of pottery spread widely beyond the actual centre of Blackduck culture, and is found together with other wares, especially in Selkirk sites. Archaeologists doubt that the broader distribution of Blackduck pottery could have been accomplished through trade, because Blackduck ware is not so superior to other local pottery that it would have been sought out. The style could have been copied, but the differences between Blackduck and Selkirk ceramics go beyond shape and surface treatment. One plausible explanation is that the Blackduck pottery in peripheral areas was made by women who, after marrying men of neighbouring tribes, had moved north and west to their husbands' homes. Such movements seem to have gone both ways, since Selkirk pottery is also found in the Blackduck core area. Intermarriage may also have contributed to family mobility across nominal tribal boundaries.

At Blackduck campsites, archaeological digs have uncovered hearths, postholes and other features, but have revealed almost nothing about the inhabitants' houses. The tools of Blackduck people are not very different from those of their immediate neighbours and of their boreal-forest antecedents. Southerly settlements, owing to contact with Eastern Woodland and Plains Indians, enjoyed a more elaborate culture than that of the bands who lived farther north. Blackduck people were probably ancestral Ojibwa.

Western Cree Prehistory

The Cree, or more precisely the Western Cree, originally lived in the boreal forest. But before Europeans reached western Canada, some of the Cree had expanded southwestwards into prairie-parkland country, where previously they had been fringe occupants. They also ranged northwards across the sparsely occupied Hudson Bay Lowlands to the Bay itself. Although the Cree are more numerous east of the Manitoba–Ontario border, they have had a substantial late-prehistoric presence in a broad zone running across central and

Plate 48. Selkirk Ceramics Two rim sherds and a small bowl are from Manitoba. The 17.4-cm-long bowl belongs to the Clearwater variety.

northern Manitoba and Saskatchewan, and just grazing Alberta. In historical times, they extended their range farther into Alberta and northward into territory previously occupied by people of the Taltheilei tradition. Their linguistic affiliation is with the Algonquian family, which includes several Subarctic tribes of eastern Canada.

In prehistoric times—before European contact—the Western Cree are identified with the distribution of Selkirk pottery, which includes several regional varieties made in a broad zone extending from northern Ontario into Alberta. Among these varieties, the widespread Clearwater Lake and more-localized Kame Hills types are found in Western Cree territory, especially in Manitoba. Occasionally, Selkirk pottery turns up farther north, where it evidently had been carried by travellers from the south.

Most implements of the Clearwater Lake and other northerly Selkirk bands were similar to those of the Blackduck people. Differences in tool kits relate more to location—whether within the boreal forest or closer to the Great Lakes and Plains—than to whether pottery remains identify the inhabitants as Selkirk or Blackduck people. Technologically and stylistically, Selkirk pottery combines elements of both Blackduck and the preceding Laurel ceramics. As we have seen, Blackduck appeared a few centuries earlier than Selkirk, and persisted up to the historical period, especially in northwestern Ontario, where it is associated with the Ojibwa, who are linguistic cousins of the Cree. To explain Selkirk origins, it is not necessary to invoke a major migration. Evidently, recombination of old and new pottery attributes is involved, along with ongoing development and local specialization. The earliest campsites containing Clearwater Lake pottery date back to 600 years ago; those with Kame Hills pottery are possibly a few centuries older. Opinions differ, however, on exactly how to reconstruct what happened in prehistory when Selkirk ceramics appeared 600 to 900 years ago, probably in central Manitoba.

Selkirk ceramics are fabric-impressed, sometimes over the entire exterior, which, when partially smoothed has a rough, lumpy appearance. Like Laurel, they have an encircling row of indented dots below the slightly flaring rim of the moderately constricted neck. These punched impressions are especially characteristic of the Clearwater Lake and Kame Hills varieties. The rim lip may also be decorated

Plate 49. Rock Paintings Of the rock paintings reproduced in this section, the two figures from a composite painting, one with bow and arrow, are from Frances Lake in northern Ontario, near the Manitoba border; the two other figures, with antenna-like projections on their heads (interpreted as portraying Manitou power), are from the Hickson-Maribelli site, Saskatchewan; and the moose is from Fishing Lake, Manitoba.

with incised or cord-impressed lines. Selkirk pots are globular, also a Blackduck characteristic, and some are slightly cone-shaped at the base, an earlier Laurel characteristic. However, their basic fabrication and decoration differ fundamentally from those of Laurel ceramics in that the coiling technique was not used to build up the walls, nor do indented designs embellish the surface. In addition to cooking pots, the Kame Hills people also made platters, cups, bowls and smoking-pipes in their home territory around Southern Indian Lake in the Churchill River drainage. It is unusual to find tobacco-smoking in the Subarctic in prehistoric times. The Kame Hills people may have adopted it from the Blackduck, who in turn got it through contact with people of the Great Lakes region.

Implements used by the Clearwater Lake and Kame Hills people to pursue their archaic hunting and fishing lifeway included the expected range of boreal-forest tools: arrow points, scrapers, spokeshaves, adze bits, ovoid-to-triangular flaked-stone knives, and whetstones. There are also grooved stone maul-heads, pebble net-sinkers and other fishing implements. Bone and antler tools are not very often found, but include antler adze bits, hide-fleshers made by shaping the end of a long ungulate leg-bone (a very widely known type), harpoon heads barbed on one side (not the toggling type), snowshoe needles, shaft straighteners used in making arrows, and bone beads. No dwellings have been excavated. The recurrent occupation of campsites clustered along waterways, as around Southern Indian Lake, points to a lifeway that focused on fishing and on hunting animals found close to the shores of lakes and rivers.

Rock Paintings

Ancestral Cree and their Ojibwa neighbours painted figures on cliff faces, near water level, along the lakes and rivers in the region extending from southwestern Quebec across northern Ontario, central Manitoba and into northern Saskatchewan. The greatest number of paintings have been found along the Churchill River, especially in Saskatchewan, in the Sturgeon–Weir river system in Manitoba, and around the Lake of the Woods. The paintings were done with the dull-red iron oxide, hematite (red ochre). Figures and motifs found in Manitoba and Saskatchewan include both realistic and stylized mammals, mythological creatures, part-human and part-bird figures,

human faces and heads, and fantastic designs. There are mythical thunderbirds, geometric designs, and snakes. People in boats are portrayed in eastern parts of the area. However, the "water panthers" sometimes portrayed in the rock paintings of northern Ontario, are absent. Recognizable animals include caribou, bison, the occasional moose, and possibly beaver. One obviously historical painting shows a man shooting a gun. Some figures are painted in outline; others are filled in. They appear as part of either a composition or a jumbled complex of figures. Individual figures may be simple or detailed.

Unquestionably, the paintings have a magic or religious significance. They may pertain to personal acts, such as vision quests, rather than to group observances. Nevertheless, the Cree reportedly performed religious ceremonies on Dance Island, a rock-painting site in Southern Indian Lake in Manitoba. Once they were made, rock paintings often became shrines, where it was common for travellers to leave tobacco or other offerings.

The rock paintings have not been accurately dated, but specialists believe that most of those that have survived predate the establishment of inland European trading posts in the region by no more than a few hundred years. The northernmost example known, located just above Lake Athabasca near Fort Smith, was made after European contact, judging from its content. Some others were also done in historical times, but the majority may be much older.

Though some of these rock paintings are found in Taltheilei or historical Athapaskan territory, especially where Cree and Athapaskans overlapped during recent centuries, ancestral Athapaskans elsewhere were little inclined to produce such art. Broadly speaking, the area where paintings are found west of Ontario coincides most closely with that of the Selkirk people, who were ancestral Cree. A secondary association exists with peoples of the Shield, because the vertical cliffs or outcrops of that region provided the artist with his canvas, a durable one that has lasted many generations.

Elsewhere in the Subarctic, any kind of rock art is extremely rare. North-central British Columbia presents a late exception. There, in a locality distant from other rock-art sites on the coast and in southern British Columbia, red pictographs appear on outcrops along the shores of lakes Stewart, Takla, Fraser and Babine. The figures are incredibly varied and include outlined, filled-in and stick figures

portraying humans, mammals, birds, fish, human faces, probable cosmological designs, bear tracks, and mythological birds and other creatures. Most are said to portray guardian spirits or events seen in dreams. They appear in panels of varied size and complexity. Local traditions indicate that these paintings were made relatively recently, well after white contact with the Carrier and Sekani Athapaskan inhabitants of the area. Unfortunately, we do not know what stimulated their production so recently.

A painted panel of human figures, found along the Tanana River near Fairbanks, Alaska, but destroyed by road building, is an enigmatic, isolated occurrence, and cannot reasonably be attributed to influences from outside the Subarctic. One may reflect on the uniqueness of this panel, whose makers must have been unaware of rock painting unless they had visited the Gulf of Alaska, several hundred kilometres distant, where Eskimos painted figures on cliffs along the shore. Somehow, the panel painters dared to do something not undertaken by their Subarctic neighbours. The rock paintings of the Canadian Shield, many of which are found outside the area covered by this book, are a singular feature of Subarctic prehistory.

8. Compendium

This book has treated prehistory on a broad, regional basis, recounting events in each of three areas in some detail. To assist the reader in tracing the individual strands through the long, tangled skein of prehistory, this chapter will provide synopses of events as they occurred across the entire Western Subarctic from earliest times.

The reader will also find a graphic distillation of these events in the front-endpaper diagram, which plots the development of prehistoric traditions through time and space.

Some 20 000 to 12 000 Years Ago

Most of Canada was covered by ice sheets during this period, separating the ice-free regions of the Northwestern Area from the rest of the continent. At times, though, there was an ice-free corridor running north and south in western Canada, through which ancestral Palaeo-Indians may have migrated southwards from Beringia, which they had reached via the Bering land-bridge that connected this continent with eastern Siberia during the last ice age. Evidence that eastern Beringia was occupied during those early millennia is limited at present to finds from the Bluefish Caves in the Yukon. Other sparse traces may have survived destruction, but have yet to be positively identified.

12 000 to 11 000 Years Ago

There is more evidence for human occupation of Beringia during this period, though it is not abundant. Stone implements made from large elongate flakes, fashioned in both the bifacial and unifacial modes, are found in sites of the Nenana complex of Alaska. At the same time, Clovis people from the south were expanding northwards into Alberta and Saskatchewan, from which the ice sheets were rapidly receding. These people were adapted to a late–Ice Age subsistence lifeway of the Plains and the spruce–poplar forest that preceded the spread of grasslands. At this time, most of the Subarctic was still covered by ice sheets.

11 000 to 10 000 Years Ago

About 11 000 years ago, or slightly later, Palaeo-Arctic microblade people reached Alaska from Siberia. Their Nenana-complex antecedents, also called Northern Cordilleran in this book, who lacked microblade technology, were moving eastwards from Beringia into northern parts of the Rocky Mountain region, from which the glaciers had retreated by the end of this period. Now linked with Beringia, the Cordilleran region was also being penetrated from the south by late fluted-point (Clovis) people, who had entered the region from northern Alberta and northwestern British Columbia. The lands east of Great Bear and Great Slave lakes and Lake Athabasca, and north and east of Lake Winnipeg, were still in the grip of the glaciers.

10 000 to 8 000 Years Ago

Nearly all of the Subarctic had emerged from the Ice Age by the end of this period. The boreal forest that had flourished there before the last ice age had become reestablished, and the climate was warmer than it is today. In the northwest, the microblade people were well established in Alaska and were spreading eastwards, though they had yet to cross the mountains into the Mackenzie drainage. One divergent branch of these microblade-using Palaeo-Arctic people colonized the North Pacific coast and may have penetrated inland locally. Nevertheless, the Northern Cordilleran population prospered without microblades in many areas, ranging from Fisherman Lake in the south to the Firth River in the northern Yukon. Plano people—the successors to Clovis—were penetrating the early boreal forest northwards from the Plains and eastwards into Ontario, but well-dated evidence for Plano people in the Subarctic is localized, and dates mainly from the next period.

8 000 to 6 000 Years Ago

The Early Palaeo-Arctic microblade tradition waned in the Northwestern Area as a result of population replacement and technological change in ongoing communities, though it survived in scattered areas. During this period, some Palaeo-Arctic people may have moved to the eastern flank of the Cordillera, but evidence for this is strongest in the next period. Northern Cordilleran people, who characteristically made lanceolate spear points, were now supplanting the microblade people in parts of the extreme northwestern interior, including Alaska. In some cases this happened through migration and population replacement, but in other cases may have been the result of technological change within existing populations. One Northern Cordilleran group, Acasta, moved eastwards north of Great Bear Lake, travelling as far as the Coppermine River. Farther east, Northern Plano people pushed into the northern limits of the Keewatin boreal forest. Some of their campsites, as at Aberdeen Lake, are now on the Barren Grounds, but the climate was warmer during this period, and the forests extended farther north than they do today.

6 000 to 4 000 Years Ago

Microblade-using people continued to inhabit parts of the Northwestern Area. One group had become established in the Mackenzie drainage, and from them the technique of making and using microblades was adopted by other peoples living east of the Cordillera in the western Northwest Territories and northern Alberta. By now, Palaeo-Arctic people were also adopting some of the implements of their neighbours, particularly those of the Northern Archaic.

Large notched points were adopted throughout the Subarctic, together with other new tool forms, signalling the development of two new cultures: the Shield in the east and the Northern Archaic in the west. The Shield culture appears to have developed out of the Northern Plano, and the Northern Archaic tradition from the Northern Cordilleran group of cultures. Though there may have been no replacement of populations, the technological and stylistic changes that occurred at this time warrant their being accorded these new names. By this time, if not earlier, lifeways in the Subarctic had probably become similar to those prevailing later, at the time of initial European contact. Climate and vegetation would have been much like those of modern times.

4 000 to 3 000 Years Ago

Up to this time, Subarctic peoples had no northern neighbours. Their high-latitude domain ended at the Arctic Ocean. Then, 4 000 years ago, ancestral Eskimos colonized the northern fringes. However, Shield, Northern Archaic, and hybrid microblade people continued to contribute to the Subarctic mosaic.

In the North-Central Area, beginning about 3 500 years ago, ancestral Eskimos, also called the Pre-Dorset, moved south as far as Lake Athabaska. The Shield people had withdrawn from the eastern part of that area, probably because of a worsening climate, and might never have encountered the new arrivals. The Palaeo-Eskimos may have been the first inhabitants of the North to use the bow and arrow, which Indians of the Subarctic do not appear to have adopted until a few centuries ago. Late Shield people continued to prosper farther south in the boreal forest, which they inhabited eastward from Saskatchewan as far as Labrador. Occupants of the lower-latitude boreal forest were influenced in their lifeways by the peoples of the Plains-Parkland transition zone and those of the Great Lakes region.

3 000 to 2 000 Years Ago

Northern Archaic people continued to occupy the Northwestern Area. There were also pockets of people whose tools combined Northern Archaic and microblade technologies, but all or nearly all of them abandoned microblades or died out by the end of the period. Central-interior British Columbia was a region of transition, showing influences from the Plateau and Plains to the south and east, as well as from the Subarctic.

Within a few centuries, the Palaeo-Eskimos withdrew from the North-Central Area. The new inhabitants of the region, who appeared there about 2 600 years ago, were the first representatives of Taltheilei tradition, and are thought to be among the ancestors of Athapaskan Indians. By the end of the period, Taltheilei people occupied an immense area from the Barren Grounds southwards into northern Alberta, Saskatchewan and Manitoba. Their origins are poorly understood, though they are thought to stem from Northern Archaic people of the Cordilleran region, among whom we expect to find the common ancestor of all Athapaskan speakers.

Though the Shield people did not return to their northern homeland, they completed their expansion into eastern Canada as far as Labrador. This may have been accomplished in part through the diffusion of Shield lifeways to immigrants from the south, especially in northeastern Ontario and Quebec. At the end of the period, ongoing development and the adoption of ceramics from the south led to the rise of the Laurel culture, particularly in parts of Manitoba and northern Ontario.

2 000 to 1 000 Years Ago

The last two millennia of Western Subarctic prehistory belong to the Athapaskan, Cree and Ojibwa Indians. But the development of historically known tribes can be traced only for the last centuries of prehistory. In the Northwestern Area, there was continuity from the Northern Archaic culture to the late prehistoric, though the style of prehistoric implements changed over time. Taltheilei people prevailed in the vast North-Central Area. Here too, the styles of tools, and especially of projectile points, changed through time. In the Eastern Area, Laurel people continued to occupy portions of the boreal forest, extending from Manitoba to western Quebec. By the end of the millennium, they were undergoing a transition into prehistoric Selkirk and Blackduck Cree and Ojibwa.

1 000 Years Ago to A.D. 1800

The Selkirk and Blackduck cultures predominated in Manitoba and northern Ontario during the final centuries of prehistory. Selkirk pottery, especially the Clearwater Lake variety, spread west through the southern boreal forest to Alberta. Its distribution accords with that of the Western Cree during historical times. The Churchill River system is seen as both a route of dissemination and an avenue of communication through which many of the dispersed ancestral Cree maintained contact with one another.

To the north and on the southern Barrens, Late Taltheilei became identified with the Yellowknife, Chipewyan, and probably also the Dogrib and Beaver tribes of Athapaskans. In the Yukon, northern British Columbia and Alaska, there were additional technological variants of late-prehistoric Athapaskan culture derived from the Northern Archaic.

In western Alaska, early Athapaskans were strongly influenced by their Eskimo neighbours. Their mode of semisubterranean house construction, use of ground slate for knives and arrow tips, and production of pottery show this influence. Conversely, the canoe-kayaks, snowshoes, and birch-bark baskets made by inland Eskimos show

Athapaskan influence. People in the western Yukon and adjacent interior Alaska made numerous implements and ornaments hammered from nuggets of native copper. They had relegated stone-knapping to a minor role, mainly for making scraper bits. The Klo-kut site and others of the northern Yukon may be considered as typical of most late-prehistoric Athapaskan groups, though perhaps no one regional culture is any more typical than any other. Another regional Athapaskan culture is represented by the protohistoric Chilcotin from central British Columbia, who occupied the northern part of the Plateau region, an area that is not dealt with in this volume. They may have moved in from the north only a few centuries earlier, but by the end of the eighteenth century had adopted some of the Plateau technology from neighbouring peoples.

We have seen that the immediate ancestors of the Athapaskans and Cree, distributed from western Alaska to Hudson Bay, display great variety in technological styles and materials, particularly between stone, copper, bone and ceramics. Perhaps cultures and regions in the more remote past were equally heterogeneous.

Appendix
Archaeological Agencies

Archaeological excavations and certain related activities in the provinces and territories are regulated by the bills and ordinances of each jurisdiction. Inquiries concerning their administration may be addressed to the agencies listed below. These agencies also receive and record heritage information reported to them by the general public as well as that derived from professional research. Conversely, they provide the public with information on archaeological research and fieldwork within their jurisdictions.

Additional information can be obtained from provincial and local museums, from university departments of anthropology and archaeology, and from the Archaeological Survey of Canada, Canadian Museum of Civilization (P.O. Box 3100, Station "B", Hull, Quebec, J8X 4H2).

Alberta
Archaeological Survey
Archaeology and Ethnology Section
Provincial Museum of Alberta
12845 - 102 Avenue
Edmonton, Alberta   T5N 0M6

British Columbia
Archaeology Branch
Ministry of Municipal Affairs, Recreation and Culture
800 Johnson Street, 5th Floor
Victoria, British Columbia   V8V IX4

Manitoba
Historic Resources Branch
Department of Culture, Heritage and Recreation
117 Lombard Avenue, 3rd Floor
Winnipeg, Manitoba   R3B 0W3

Northwest Territories
Prince of Wales Northern Heritage Centre
Government of the Northwest Territories
Yellowknife, NWT   XIA 2L9

Saskatchewan
Heritage Branch
Culture, Multiculturalism and Recreation
3211 Albert Street
Regina, Saskatchewan   S4S 5W6

Yukon Territory
Heritage Branch
Yukon Tourism
Government of the Yukon
P.O. Box 2703
Whitehorse, Yukon   YIA 2C6

Annotated Reading List

Publications on Subarctic prehistory have been written almost exclusively for specialists. Among them are innumerable reports on local areas but relatively few that attempt to give comprehensive coverage. Some of the less-specialized publications, plus a few more-technical ones, are listed below; these, in turn, contain further references to specialized or regional literature, including monographs reporting on archaeological excavations.

Carlisle, Ronald C., comp. and ed.
(1988) *Americans before Columbus: Ice-Age origins.* University of Pittsburgh, Department of Anthropology, Ethnology Monographs, no. 12. Pittsburgh, Pa.

Though of indirect relevance to the Subarctic, this compilation of papers from the First Columbian Quincentenary Symposium, Smithsonian Institution, describes Ice Age conditions in North America, changes in geography and vegetation, and animal extinctions at the end of the Ice Age. It also presents the case for and against pre-Clovis migrations.

Derry, David E., and Douglas R. Hudson, eds.
(1975) *Athapaskan archaeology.* The Western Canadian Journal of Anthropology 5, nos. 3–4. Edmonton: University of Alberta Department of Anthropology.

The focus of the nine articles in this special issue ranges from topical (for example, migration, the fur trade) to regional (interior Alaska) and local (the Karpinsky site in Alberta).

Dewdney, Selwyn, and Kenneth E. Kidd
(1967) *Indian rock paintings of the Great Lakes.* 2d ed. Toronto: University of Toronto Press for the Quetico Foundation.

Remains a primary study of rock paintings and source for their locations.

Epp, Henry T., and Ian Dyck, eds.
(1983) *Tracking ancient hunters: Prehistoric archaeology in Saskatchewan.* Regina: Saskatchewan Archaeological Society.

A chapter by David Meyer deals with the prehistory of northern Saskatchewan. Other instructive chapters describe archaeological methods.

Fladmark, Knut R.
(1986) *British Columbia prehistory.* (Canadian Prehistory Series). Ottawa: National Museums of Canada, National Museum of Man.

Though not primarily concerned with the province's subarctic region, the book touches briefly on that aspect of British Columbia prehistory.

(1985) *Glass and ice: The archaeology of Mt. Edziza.* Simon Fraser University Department of Archaeology, Publication no. 14. Burnaby, B. C.

A study of an important source of obsidian and its associated flaking stations in northern British Columbia, from which this volcanic rock was widely traded.

Franklin, U.M., E. Badone, R. Gotthardt, and B. Yorga
(1981) *An examination of prehistoric copper technology and copper sources in western arctic and subarctic North America.* National Museum of Man Mercury Series, Archaeological Survey of Canada Paper no. 101. Ottawa: National Museums of Canada.

This is the principal source of information for the section on copper working technology in Chapter 6 of the present volume.

Gordon, Bryan C.
(1981) "Man-environment relationships in Barrenland prehistory." *Musk-Ox* 28: 1–19.

The primary source for the prehistory of the Barren Grounds of the Keewatin-Mackenzie districts. It studies the location and definition of prehistoric peoples in relation to discrete caribou herds.

Hearne, Samuel
(1795) *A journey from Prince of Wales's Fort, in Hudson's Bay, to the northern ocean … in the years 1769, 1770, 1771 & 1772*. London. Reprinted Toronto: Macmillan, 1958; Edmonton: Hurtig, 1971.

Contains accounts of Indian life on the Barren Grounds early in the period of European contact.

Helmer, J.W., S. van Dyke, and F.J. Kense, eds.
(1977) *Problems in the prehistory of the North American subarctic; the Athapaskan question*. Calgary: Archaeological Association, Department of Archaeology, University of Calgary.

Most of the twenty-seven articles in these proceedings of the 9th annual conference of the Association are on archaeological topics, but some also describe physical anthropology and post-contact culture change.

Historical Atlas of Canada
(1987) "Prehistory." Sec. 1 of Vol. 1, *From the beginning to 1800*, edited by R. Cole Harris, cartography by Geoffrey J. Matthews, pp. 1–6, pls. 1–18. Toronto: University of Toronto Press.

Canada's prehistory is summarized and illustrated in a series of maps and texts by James V. Wright and others.

Ives, John W.
(1981) "The prehistory of the boreal forest of northern Alberta." In *Alberta archaeology; prospect and retrospect*, edited by T.A. Moore, 39–58. Lethbridge, Alberta: Archaeological Society of Alberta.

Describes the ecology and environment of the region, and provides a detailed report on research done to date of publication. The results of fieldwork are conservatively interpreted, and they do not provide sufficient basis for a reconstruction of northern Alberta prehistory.

Jones, Tim E.H.
(1981) *The aboriginal rock paintings of the Churchill River*. Saskatchewan Museum of Natural History, Anthropological Series, no. 4. Regina: Saskatchewan Department of Culture and Youth.

Documents and analyses the sites in the Saskatchewan area of the river.

Le Blanc, Raymond Joseph
(1984) *The Rat Indian Creek site and the late prehistoric period in the interior northern Yukon*. National Museum of Man Mercury Series, Archaeological Survey of Canada Paper no. 120. Ottawa: National Museums of Canada.

This site report describes and analyses a large excavated assemblage of artifacts from the last 2 000 years.

MacNeish, Richard S.
(1964) "Archaeological investigations, comparisons and speculation." In *Investigations in southwest Yukon*. Papers of the Robert S. Peabody Foundation for Archaeology, Vol. 6, no. 2. Andover, Mass.

A pioneer work of data reporting, together with an ambitious reconstruction of northwestern North American prehistory. The author's conclusions have since been greatly expanded and emended by later research.

Meyer, David, and Dale Russell
(1987) "The Selkirk composite of central Canada: a reconsideration." *Arctic Anthropology* 24(2):1–31.

Defines and compares the several phases of the Selkirk tradition (apparent ancestral Cree) and considers their origins.

Morlan, Richard E., and Jacques Cinq-Mars
(1982) "Ancient Beringians: human occupations in the Late Pleistocene of Alaska and the Yukon Territory". In *Paleoecology of Beringia*, edited by David M. Hopkins et al., 353–81. New York: Academic Press.

A summary of the research on the earliest occupation of the Subarctic and the sometimes controversial data, and an account of the discoveries in the Bluefish Caves.

Morlan, Richard E., and William B. Workman
(1980) "Prehistoric man in the southwest Yukon." In *Kluane, pinnacle of the Yukon*, edited by John B. Theberge, 97–107. Toronto: Doubleday.

Pettipas, Leo F., ed.
(1983) *Introducing Manitoba prehistory*. Papers in Manitoba Archaeology, Popular Series no. 4. Manitoba Department of Cultural Affairs and Historical Resources.

Assembled papers on the prehistory of the boreal-forest region of Manitoba, and the interpretation of ancient lifeways.

Russell, Dale Ronald
(1991) *The eighteenth-century Western Cree and their neighbours*. Canadian Museum of Civilization Mercury Series, Archaeological Survey of Canada Paper no. 143.

This substantial survey of historical documents helps to bridge the gulf between Western Cree prehistory, early historical inhabitants of the region west of Ontario, and the Indian groups documented during the nineteenth century. By 1700, Crees were living as far west as central Alberta, but six Cree groups on the Plains, in the Parkland and in the boreal forest were obliterated by the smallpox epidemic of 1871, only to be replaced during the 1800s by others who shifted into the areas that they had occupied.

Smithsonian Institution
(1981) *Handbook of North American Indians. Vol. 6, Subarctic*, edited by June Helm. Washington, D.C.

A compendium of articles by experts in their fields on the prehistory of North America, broken down by regions. Numerous articles describe the indigenous tribes of the regions and their history. This major reference work is not overly technical, and thus is comfortably accessible to the lay reader.

Steegmann, Jr., A. Theodore, ed.
(1983) *Boreal forest adaptations: the Northern Algonkians*. New York: Plenum Press.

Various authors describe the ecology, prehistory and early-historical cultural change in the region, with emphasis on the particular problems of life in the boreal forest of northern Ontario.

Steinbring, Jack, and Maurice Lanteigne
(1989) *An overview of rock art research in Canada*. The Rock Art Association of Manitoba Newsletter 2(2):2–5.

The newsletter also contains a comprehensive bibliography, beginning on page 6, that may be especially useful.

Wright, James V.
(1972) *Ontario prehistory, an eleven-thousand-year archaeological outline*. (Canadian Prehistory Series). Ottawa: National Museum of Man, National Museums of Canada. Reprinted Scarborough, Ont.: Van Nostrand Reinhold.

Discusses the more highly developed prehistoric cultures of the Great Lakes region, whose influence reached adjacent subarctic areas, and briefly describes the prehistory of subarctic northern and northwestern Ontario.

(1972) *The Shield Archaic*. National Museum of Man, Publications in Archaeology no. 3. Ottawa: National Museums of Canada.

Defines the Shield culture, within both the subarctic area covered by the present volume and the rest of Ontario and eastern Canada.